CONTENTS

CHAPTER 1 • Place Value and Number Sense

Numbers in Your World 1

Build to Thousands 2

Thousands 3

Compare and Order Numbers 4

Problem-Solving Strategy: Make a Table 5

Round Numbers 6

Millions 7

Problem Solving: Interpret Data 8

CHAPTER 2 • Money, Addition, and Subtraction

Count Money and Make Change 9

Compare, Order, and Round Money 10

Mental Math: Addition Strategies 11

Mental Math: Estimate Sums 12

Add Whole Numbers 13

Three or More Addends 14

Mental Math: Subtraction Strategies 15

Mental Math: Estimate Differences 16

Subtract Whole Numbers 17

Problem-Solving Strategy: Choose the Operation 18

Subtract Across Zero 19

Problem Solving: Find Needed or Extra Information 20

CHAPTER 3 • Time, Data, and Graphs

Time 21

Elapsed Time 22

Problem-Solving Strategy: Work Backward 23

Range, Median, and Mode 24

Pictographs 25

Bar Graphs 26

Ordered Pairs 27

Line Graphs 28

Problem Solving: Interpret Data 29

CHAPTER 4 • Multiplication and Division Facts

Meaning of Multiplication 30

Mental Math: 2 Through 5 as Factors 31

Mental Math: 6 and 8 as Factors 32

Mental Math: 7 and 9 as Factors 33

Problem-Solving Strategy: Find a Pattern 34

Three Factors 35

Meaning of Division 36

2 Through 5 as Divisors 37

6 Through 9 as Divisors 38

Fact Families 39

Remainders 40

Problem Solving: Choose the Operation 41

CHAPTER 5 • Multiply by 1-Digit Numbers

Mental Math: Multiplication Patterns 42

Mental Math: Estimate Products 43

Use Models to Multiply 44

Multiply 2-Digit Numbers 45

Problem-Solving Strategy:
Solve Multistep Problems 46

Multiply Greater Numbers 47

Multiply with Money 48

Problem Solving: Interpret Data 49

CHAPTER 6 • Multiply 2-Digit Numbers

Mental Math: Multiplication Patterns 50

Mental Math: Estimate Products 51

Multiply 2-Digit Numbers 52

Multiply 2-Digit Numbers 53

Problem-Solving Strategy: Use Alternate
Solution Methods 54

Multiply 3-Digit Numbers and Money 55

Multiply Greater Numbers 56

Problem Solving: Use an Estimate or
Find the Exact Answer 57

CHAPTER 7 • Measurement

Length in Customary Units 58

Rename Customary Units of Length 59

Length in Metric Units 60

Perimeter 61

Capacity and Weight in Customary Units 62

Problem Solving: Use Logical Reasoning 63

Capacity and Mass in Metric Units 64

Problem Solving: Check for Reasonableness 65

CHAPTER 8 • Divide by 1- and 2-Digit Numbers

Mental Math: Division Patterns 66

Mental Math: Estimate Quotients 67

Division by 1-Digit Numbers 68

Division by 1-Digit Numbers 69

Zeros in the Quotient 70

Divide Greater Numbers 71

Problem-Solving Strategy: Guess, Test, and Revise 72

Average 73

Mental Math: Divide by Multiples of Ten 74

Divide by Tens 75

Problem Solving: Interpret the Quotient
and Remainder 76

CHAPTER 9 • Geometry

3-Dimensional Figures 77

2-Dimensional Figures and Polygons 78

Line Segments, Lines, and Rays 79

Problem-Solving Strategy: Make an Organized List 80

Angles 81

Congruency and Similarity 82

Symmetry 83

Slides, Flips, and Turns 84

Area 85

Volume 86

Problem Solving: Use Diagrams 87

CHAPTER 10 • Fractions and Probability

Part of a Whole 88

Part of a Group 89

Find a Fraction of a Number 90

Equivalent Fractions 91

Simplify Fractions 92

Compare Fractions 93

Mixed Numbers 94

Probability 95

Fractions and Probability 96

Problem-Solving Strategy:
Conduct an Experiment 97

Predict and Experiment 98

Problem Solving:
Solve Multistep Problems 99

CHAPTER 11 • Using Fractions

Add Fractions 100

Add Fractions 101

Subtract Fractions 102

Subtract Fractions 103

Find a Common Denominator 104

Add and Subtract Fractions with Unlike Denominators 105

Problem-Solving Strategy: Draw a Picture 106

Add and Subtract Mixed Numbers 107

Problem Solving: Choose the Operation 108

CHAPTER 12 • Decimals

Decimals Less Than 1 109

Decimals Greater Than 1 110

Compare and Order Decimals 111

Problem-Solving Strategy: Solve a Simpler Problem 112

Mental Math: Estimate Sums and Differences 113

Add and Subtract Decimals 114

Add Decimals 115

Subtract Decimals 116

Problem Solving: Write a Number Sentence 117

NUMBERS IN YOUR WORLD

Write a sentence in which the number is used in the way given.

1. 97, used to show order _____

2. 19, used to show measure _____

3. 101, used to name _____

4. 12, used to show measure _____

5. 48, used to count _____

6. 35, used to show order _____

7. 202, used to name _____

8. 550, used to count _____

9. 180, used to show measure _____

10. Write four sentences about your favorite sports. Use numbers to count, order, name, and measure.

_____

_____

11. Write four sentences about how you spend your weekend or summer. Use numbers to count, order, name, and measure.

_____

_____

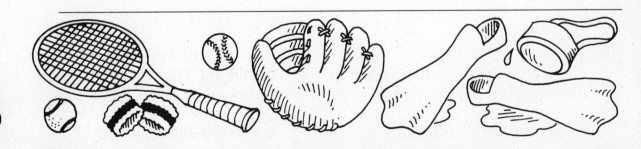

BUILD TO THOUSANDS

Write the number.

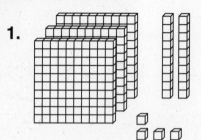

1. _____   2. _____   3. _____

4. 8 hundreds 6 tens 2 ones _____   5. 5 hundreds 3 tens 9 ones_____

6. 1 thousand 3 tens 4 ones _____   7. 1 thousand 2 hundreds _____

8. 1 thousand, 3 tens _____   9. 6 thousands, 9 ones _____

10. 32 tens 9 ones _____   11. 126 tens 7 ones _____

12. 90 tens _____   13. 44 tens _____

Complete the table.

	Number	Thousands	Hundreds	Tens	Ones
14.	436				
15.			6	9	2
16.	1,748				
17.	1,043				

Solve.

18. There are 468 reference books and 1,000 more picture books in the library. How many picture books are there? _____

19. There are 657 animal books in the library. There are 100 more books about plants. How many books are about plants? _____

Practice **3**

THOUSANDS

Write the number in standard form and in expanded form.

1.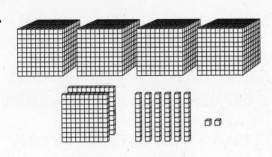

_____

_____

2.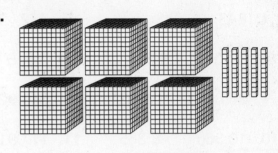

_____

_____

3. eight hundred ninety _____

4. fourteen thousand fifty-eight _____

5. six hundred four thousand, six _____

6. three hundred thousand twenty _____

Write the word name for the number.

7. 3,524 _____

8. 23,086 _____

9. 423,500 _____

Solve.

10. Richard sold 255 baseball cards to Tino. Write the word form and expanded form of this number.

_____

_____

11. The baseball card store owns two hundred twenty thousand, nine hundred eighty-five cards. Write this number in standard form.

_____

COMPARE AND ORDER NUMBERS

Compare. Write >, <, or =.

1. 643 ◯ 943   **2.** 472 ◯ 427   **3.** 1,000 ◯ 10,000

4. 5,107 ◯ 5,211   **5.** 7,316 ◯ 7,309   **6.** 2,134 ◯ 2,116

7. 30,821 ◯ 31,821   **8.** 643,927 ◯ 697,625   **9.** 203,497 ◯ 20,349

10. 10,365 ◯ 8,365   **11.** 11,091 ◯ 11,901   **12.** 97,000 ◯ 89,999

13. 65,212 ◯ 56,212   **14.** 28,545 ◯ 28,545   **15.** 56,619 ◯ 56,916

Order the numbers from least to greatest.

16. 429; 306; 489 _____

17. 4,507; 2,698; 2,664 _____

18. 8,543; 4,876; 4,856 _____

19. 9,862; 98,438; 98,135 _____

20. 14,320; 8,940; 13,098 _____

21. 56,324; 55,873; 55,818 _____

22. 657,563; 675,843; 657,365 _____

23. 345,713; 445,713; 234,713 _____

24. 716,049; 716,490; 716,029 _____

Solve.

25. There are 325 fourth graders and 340 fifth graders participating in a contest. Which grade has more participants?

26. The fourth graders scored the following points: 87, 112, 98, 126, 95. Rank these points from least to greatest.

_____   _____

McGraw-Hill School Division

PROBLEM-SOLVING STRATEGY: MAKE A TABLE

Solve using the make-a-table strategy.

1. Pam, Tim, and Alex are reporting on one different sports figure each. Tim does not choose Matt Biondi or Larry Bird. Pam does not choose Matt Biondi. Which sports figure does Alex choose?

	Biondi	Bjurstedt	Bird
Pam			
Tim			
Alex			

_____

2. Each athlete plays a different sport. Larry Bird does not swim or play tennis. Matt Biondi swims. What sport does Molla Bjurstedt play?

	Bird	Bjurstedt	Biondi
basketball			
tennis			
swimming			

_____

Solve using any method.

3. Molla Bjurstedt won her first U.S. championship in 1915. Matt Biondi won his in 1984. Whose championship was almost 100 years ago?

_____

4. Basketball player Larry Bird played in 897 regular season games. He had 8,974 rebounds and 5,695 assists. Did he have more assists or rebounds?

_____

5. Matt Biondi has won 11 Olympic medals for swimming. He has 4 times as many gold medals as silver medals. He has twice as many silver medals as bronze medals. How many of each type has he won?

_____

6. There were 2,278 fans at a swim meet. There were 2,267 fans at a tennis match. Which had more fans, the swim meet or the tennis match?

_____

ROUND NUMBERS

Complete the table.

		Round to the nearest ten.	Round to the nearest hundred.	Round to the nearest thousand.
1.	2,648			
2.	7,421			
3.	68,725			
4.	34,293			
5.	387,843			
6.	506,027			

7. Algebra Find the rule. Then complete the table.

Rule:	
Input	**Output**
45,897	46,897
1,324	2,324
543,918	544,918
45,715	
67,159	
876,532	

Rule:	
Input	**Output**
17,540	7,540
85,342	75,342
791,247	781,247
54,671	
178,419	
732,696	

Rule:	
Input	**Output**
7,632	7,630
56,167	56,170
5,134	5,130
98,723	
185,784	
678,186	

Solve.

8. There were 10,287 people watching the contest. What is this number rounded to the nearest hundred?

9. There were 1,876 people in the contest. What is this number rounded to the nearest ten?

_____

_____

McGraw-Hill School Division

MILLIONS

Complete the different names for the number.

1. 30,000 = _____ thousands or _____ ten thousands

2. 200,000 = _____ thousands or _____ ten thousands or

   _____ hundred thousands

3. 7,000,000 = _____ thousands or _____ ten thousands or

   _____ hundred thousands

Complete the table.

	Standard Form	Expanded Form	Word Name
4.	643,918	600,000 + 40,000 + 3,000 + 900 + 10 + 8	
5.	504,108		
6.		300,000 + 9	three hundred thousand, nine
7.		7,000,000 + 200,000 + 60,000 + 5,000 + 10 + 3	seven million, two hundred sixty-five thousand, thirteen
8.	1,423,000		
9.	5,000,362		

Solve.

10. At a stamp and card store, there were 3,496,581 baseball cards sold. In what place is the 3 in the number?

_____

11. There were 6,485,073 stamps sold at the stamp and card store. What is the value of the 4 in this number?

_____

PROBLEM SOLVING: INTERPRET DATA

✔	Read
✔	Plan
✔	Solve
✔	Look Back

Students in Ms. Hill's class compared their heights. They used a line plot to show the data. Solve using the line plot.

1. How many students are in the

class? _____

2. How many students are between

55 and 57 inches tall? _____

3. How many students are shorter

than 55 inches? _____

4. Write a sentence about what this data tells you. _____

_____

Students' Heights in Inches

				X				
			X	X	X			
X			X	X	X	X	X	
X	X	X	X	X	X	X	X	X
51	52	53	54	55	56	57	58	59

Solve using any method.

5. Mel is drawing flowers. The first flower is 2 inches tall, the second 4 inches, the third 8 inches. If Mel follows this pattern, how tall will her next three flowers be?

_____

6. **Logical Reasoning** The digits in the number are 9, 2, 1, and 3. If you round the number to the nearest hundred, you get 1,300. The digit in the tens place is 9. What's the number?

_____

7. Of the 1,293 students, about 1,000 are in all the grades except 4th grade. About how many students are in 4th grade?

_____

8. Jan's poster is 1 foot taller than Tim's poster and 3 feet taller than Hal's. Pat's is 1 foot taller than Hal's. List the posters from tallest to shortest.

_____

McGraw-Hill School Division

Name: _____

COUNT MONEY AND MAKE CHANGE

Write the money amount.

1.

_____

2.

_____

3.

_____

4.

_____

5.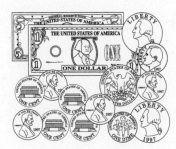

_____

6.

_____

Find the amount of change.

7. Cost: 36¢
   Amount given: $1.00

   _____

8. Cost: $3.60
   Amount given: $5.00

   _____

9. Cost: $1.03
   Amount given: $10.00

   _____

Solve.

10. Ernestine goes shopping for gifts for her family. She buys a doll for $8.95. How much change does she get back from $10.00?

    _____

11. What are two ways Ari could show 88¢ in change?

    _____

    _____

    _____

COMPARE, ORDER, AND ROUND MONEY

Write in order from least to greatest.

1. $9.80, $8.90, $9.98 _____

2. $33.50, $29.50, $602.50 _____

3. $8,203, $5,807, $5,817 _____

4. $23.98, $465.23, $347.76, $238.65 _____

5. $3,345.40, $3,256.40, $3,767.40 _____

6. $2,378.42, $2,678.42, $2,234.73 _____

Round.

7. $2.35 to the nearest dollar _____   **8.** $7.95 to the nearest dollar _____

9. $23.99 to the nearest dollar   **10.** $24.37 to the nearest dollar

_____   _____

11. $0.18 to the nearest 10¢ _____   **12.** $4.23 to the nearest 10¢ _____

13. $16.76 to the nearest 10¢ _____   **14.** $24.32 to the nearest 10¢ _____

15. $8.70 to the nearest $10 _____   **16.** $67.34 to the nearest $10 _____

17. $13.98 to the nearest $10 _____   **18.** $87.34 to the nearest $10 _____

Solve.

19. Sam has $1,045 in his savings account. Lisa has $1,134 in her savings account. Who has more money saved?

20. Sam bought a stamp for $12.67. What is this amount rounded to the nearest dollar?

_____

_____

McGraw-Hill School Division

MENTAL MATH: ADDITION STRATEGIES

Add mentally.

1. 42 + 35 = _____

2. 61 + 24 = _____

3. 33 + 15 = _____

4. 44 + 42 = _____

5. 58 + 21 = _____

6. 77 + 11 = _____

7. 85 + 12 = _____

8. 45 + 33 = _____

9. 24 + 45 = _____

10. 630 + 314 = _____

11. 791 + 208 = _____

12. $156 + $322 = _____

13. $555 + $333 = _____

14. $175 + $124 = _____

15. $724 + $162 = _____

Algebra Complete. Use mental math.

16. 26 + _____ = 77

17. _____ + 162 = 869

18. $555 + _____ = $798

19. _____ + $145 = $249

20. 160 + _____ = 292

21. _____ + $767 = $899

22. $525 + _____ = $956

23. _____ + 203 = 807

Solve.

24. There are 33 boys and 34 girls at the dance. How many students are there in all?

_____

25. The dance committee spent $216 on refreshments and $123 on decorations. How much did it spend?

_____

MENTAL MATH: ESTIMATE SUMS

Estimate. Round to the nearest

1. ten: 11 + 19 _____

2. ten cents: $0.67 + $0.23 _____

3. ten: 57 + 23 _____

4. ten cents: $0.94 + $0.56 _____

5. ten: 103 + 59 _____

6. ten: 24 + 67 + 43 _____

7. hundred: 495 + 313 _____

8. hundred: 777 + 722 _____

9. dollar: $4.95 + $2.10 _____

10. dollar: $9.25 + $8.95 _____

11. hundred: 3,765 + 234 _____

12. hundred: 528 + 78 + 142 _____

13. thousand: 3,965 + 2,100 _____

14. ten dollars: $15.95 + $4.25 _____

15. ten dollars: $156.87 + $36.56 _____

16. thousand: 5,923 + 569 + 234 _____

Estimate. Tell how you rounded.

17. 47 + 32

18. $.07 + $0.28

_____

_____

19. $389 + $67 + $12

20. 2,987 + 458

_____

_____

Solve.

21. Ramon wants to buy his mother flowers for $7.50 and a book for $21.95. About how much will he spend?

_____

22. Ramon's mother plants 37 tulip bulbs and 22 daffodil bulbs. About how many bulbs does she plant in all?

_____

ADD WHOLE NUMBERS

Add. Remember to estimate.

1. 42
   + 21

2. 48
   + 21

3. 26
   + 35

4. $89
   + 12

5. 32
   + 29

6. 287
   + 21

7. $6.43
   + 2.21

8. 738
   + 65

9. 579
   + 391

10. $3.89
   + 0.45

11. 2,019
   + 1,308

12. 2,908
   + 26

13. 1,256
   + 1,168

14. 2,124
   + 2,999

15. 7,236
   + 999

16. 36,413
   + 12,236

17. 68,281
   + 12,712

18. 23,786
   + 4,993

19. 12,362
   + 43,748

20. 37,689
   + 7,777

21. 233,317
   + 142,462

22. 683,924
   + 15,234

23. 562,296
   + 228,421

24. 197,243
   + 35,237

25. 297,152
   + 434,508

26. $745 + $26 = _____

27. 2,165 + 453 = _____

28. 7,621 + 1,296 = _____

29. 8,453 + 3,675 = _____

30. $34,654 + $2,398 = _____

31. 349,168 + 265,722 = _____

Solve.

32. There were 2,434 people who attended the opening of a new store on Saturday. On Sunday 1,846 people went to the store. How many people went to the store on its first weekend?

_____

33. The new store took in $110,158 the first week and $98,673 in the second week. How much did it take in during both weeks?

_____

THREE OR MORE ADDENDS

Add. Remember to estimate.

1.	12	2.	$14	3.	12	4.	26
	14		82		21		32
	+ 22		+ 3		+ 39		+ 65

5.	213	6.	721	7.	$895	8.	263
	142		20		511		192
	+ 324		+ 219		+ 345		+ 859

9.	$32.32	10.	8,239	11.	4,320	12.	3,121
	14.53		1,534		1,290		7,383
	+ 20.10		+ 121		3,860		2,947
					+ 2,199		+ 11,231

13. 61 + 69 + 33 = _____

14. 24 + 33 + 73 = _____

15. 252 + 514 + 115 = _____

16. $13.24 + $6.57 + $18.36 = _____

17. 26 + 2,300 + 765 = _____

18. $263.54 + $54.67 + $582.41 =

_____

19. 1,599 + 999 + 12,822 = _____

20. 10,340 + 4,235 + 2,378 = _____

Solve.

21. Mrs. Endo bought three items at the store. The prices were $1.12, $9.99, and $6.02. How much did she spend altogether?

_____

22. At the store, 125 people bought a sale item on Monday, 42 on Tuesday, and 37 on Wednesday. How many people bought the sale item on these three days?

_____

McGraw-Hill School Division

MENTAL MATH: SUBTRACTION STRATEGIES

Subtract mentally.

1. 36 − 8 = _____   **2.** 41 − 9 = _____   **3.** 59 − 19 = _____

4. 82 − 55 = _____   **5.** 26¢ − 15¢ = _____   **6.** 92 − 45 = _____

7. 73 − 45 = _____   **8.** 49 − 17 = _____   **9.** 71¢ − 59¢ = _____

10. 68¢ − 15¢ = _____   **11.** 34 − 12 = _____   **12.** 67 − 49 = _____

13. 45 − 27 = _____   **14.** 62 − 56 = _____   **15.** 73 − 59 = _____

16. 974 − 150 = _____   **17.** $3.75 − $2.54 = _____

18. $2.31 − $1.10 = _____   **19.** 755 − 245 = _____

20. $8.45 − $1.55 = _____   **21.** 235 − 129 = _____

22. 743 − 297 = _____   **23.** 487 − 126 = _____

24. 393 − 85 = _____   **25.** $5.07 − $0.75 = _____

26. $6.67 − $5.59 = _____   **27.** 452 − 429 = _____

28. 878 − 534 = _____   **29.** $9.85 − 0.63 = _____

Solve.

30. Kelly has saved all year for bird-watching binoculars. She finally has $126. At the store she discovers that the price has just been raised to $149. How much more will Kelly have to save?

_____

31. Kelly goes to the zoo to see the birds. There are 125 species of birds and 87 are from the area where she lives. How many birds are not from where she lives?

_____

MENTAL MATH: ESTIMATE DIFFERENCES

Estimate. Round to the nearest

1. ten: 62 − 37 _____

2. ten cents: $0.55 − $0.28 _____

3. ten cents: $0.69 − $0.41 _____

4. ten: 44 − 32 _____

5. ten: 587 − 42 _____

6. ten: 654 − 23 _____

7. hundred: 613 − 385 _____

8. hundred: 895 − 289 _____

9. hundred: 569 − 226 _____

10. dollar: $45.78 − $12.97 _____

11. dollar: $52.35 − $17.04 _____

12. thousand: 8,099 − 3,748 _____

13. ten dollars: $23.76 − $13.76

14. ten dollars: $76.98 − $8.54

_____

_____

15. thousand: 6,453 − 1,298

16. ten dollars: $62.98 − $4.65

_____

_____

17. thousand: 3,217 − 1,199

18. thousand: 3,275 − 1,716

_____

_____

Solve.

19. On vacation, Todd's family spent $57.36 on meals on the first day and $46.78 on the second. About how much less did they spend on the second day?

_____

_____

20. Todd's family drove 334 miles to the beach last year and 425 miles this year. About how much more did they drive this year?

_____

_____

McGraw-Hill School Division

SUBTRACT WHOLE NUMBERS

Subtract. Remember to estimate.

1.	87 − 31	2.	85 − 29	3.	578 − 159	4.	830 − 799

5.	7,987 − 2,174	6.	$3,659 − 1,192	7.	$7,215 − 2,875	8.	$15.25 − 3.75

9.	$15.05 − 9.50	10.	$29.95 − 16.99	11.	$17.50 − 8.99	12.	25,286 − 11,972

13.	33,749 − 14,182	14.	86,219 − 28,103	15.	$198.15 − 109.50	16.	$7,239 − 5,777

17. $20.50 − $11.00 = _____

18. $42.34 − $10.95 = _____

19. $18.92 − $9.45 = _____

20. $56.25 − $18.95 = _____

Algebra Find the missing number.

21. 68 + _____ = 132

22. _____ − 453 = 329

23. 738 − 256 = _____

24. 59 + 67 + _____ = 149

25. _____ + 456 = 925

26. 972 − _____ = 698

Solve.

27. Michelle bought 85 tickets for rides at the carnival. If she used 56 tickets, how many did she have left?

_____

28. Lee spent $6.50 on tickets for rides at the carnival. He spent the rest of his money on games. If he had $8.75 at the start of the carnival, how much did he spend on games?

_____

PROBLEM-SOLVING STRATEGY: CHOOSE THE OPERATION

✔ **Read**
✔ **Plan**
✔ **Solve**
✔ **Look Back**

Solve. Then write *add* or *subtract* to tell which operation you used.

1. Lauren and her family drove to the clothing store. When they left home the car odometer read 859 miles. When they returned, it read 875. How many miles did they drive?

_____

2. Lauren buys a jacket that costs $39 and a pair of slacks that costs $43. How much money does Lauren spend?

_____

3. Lauren buys a shirt for $8.99. She gives the clerk a $10 bill. What change does she receive?

_____

4. Lauren decides to buy a raincoat that is $10.55 less than a winter jacket. If the winter jacket is $98.99, how much does the raincoat cost?

_____

Solve using any method.

5. Bill and his family drive to the mountains to go camping. They spend $35.50 on gas, $4.75 on oil, and $79.95 on a new tire. How much does it cost them to travel?

6. Bill and his sister go fishing. They each catch 3 trout and 2 salmon. How many fish do they catch in all?

_____

7. For each of three days, Bill's family goes hiking for 5 hours, swimming for 2 hours, and fishing for 3 hours. In three days, how many hours do they spend doing these activities?

_____

8. In the mountains, the average temperature is 67°F during the day and 43°F at night. Estimate the difference between the average day and night temperatures.

_____

McGraw-Hill School Division

Name: _____

SUBTRACT ACROSS ZERO

Subtract. Remember to estimate.

1.   780
    − 241

2.   702
    − 23

3.   500
    − 236

4.   600
    − 151

5. $60.08
    − 13.23

6.   7,067
    − 3,241

7.   5,200
    − 2,035

8.   9,000
    − 643

9. $96.00
    − 43.34

10.   2,030
    − 1,304

11. $30.20
    − 2.49

12.   7,000
    − 2,415

13. $60.05
    − 14.20

14.   5,200
    − 1,745

15. $40.40
    − 9.99

16.   8,004
    − 352

17. 300 − 183 = _____

18. 750 − 246 = _____

19. 1,000 − 527 = _____

20. 1,600 − 999 = _____

21. $60.00 − $34.26 = _____

22. 3,020 − 1,564 = _____

23. 8,000 − 439 = _____

24. 800 − 243 = _____

Solve.

25. Ricardo had $15.00 when he went to the amusement park. He had $8.35 left at the end of the day. How much did he spend?

_____

26. Ricardo needs 1,000 points to win the dart game at the amusement park. If he scores 720 on his first two shots, how many more points does he need to win?

_____

McGraw-Hill School Division

PROBLEM SOLVING: FIND NEEDED OR EXTRA INFORMATION

✔ Read
✔ Plan
✔ Solve
✔ Look Back

Solve or tell what information is needed to solve the problem.
Cross out any extra information.

1. The fourth grade runs a school store. Last week the students had a profit of $137. This week they have a profit of $98. Jeff alone made $59. What was the fourth grade's profit for these weeks?

_____

2. The students sell cameras for $16. Last week one parent bought 7 cameras. Today the students sold 4 cameras. How much did they get for the cameras sold today?

_____

3. If the students sell about 4 cameras each school day for a month, about how much money will they take in at the end of the month?

_____

_____

_____

4. The students sell 23 cameras during Week 1 of September, 28 cameras during Week 2, and 18 cameras during Week 3. The fifth grade bought 16 cameras in September. About how many cameras do the students sell in September?

_____

_____

Solve using any method.

5. In the school store, a sixth grader buys two gliders at $0.57 each, one camera for $16, and sunglasses for $1.50. What change does she get from $20?

_____

6. After closing the store, Tess and Nuru count 6 $10 bills, 2 $5 bills, 13 $1 bills, 20 dimes, 4 nickels, and 30 pennies. How much money do they have?

_____

TIME

Write the time in two different ways.

1.

2.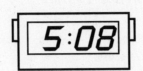

3.

_____   _____   _____

_____   _____   _____

Choose the most reasonable unit of time. Write *seconds,*
minutes, hours, days, or *weeks.*

4. Travis spends 20 _____
at the dentist.

5. The fourth grade is in school

for 6 _____.

6. Ella walks to the store in 10

_____.

7. There are 48 hours in

2 _____.

8. Angela can run nonstop for 30

_____.

9. Sophie swims underwater for 30

_____.

10. Elmore gets paid every two

_____.

11. Van hikes for 2 _____
every Saturday morning.

Solve.

12. Tim walked to the store in 20
minutes and shopped for an
hour. Then he walked home in 30
minutes. Did he spend more time
walking or shopping?

_____

13. Tim spent 55 minutes cooking
dinner and then ate his dinner in
1 hour. Did he spend more time
eating or cooking?

_____

ELAPSED TIME

Tell what time it will be:

1. in 25 min.

_____

2. in 2 h 10 min.

_____

3. in 4 h 35 min.

_____

4. 1 h 20 min after 10:40. _____

5. 45 min after 2:50. _____

6. 30 min after 6:45 P.M.

7. 1 h 45 min after 8:30 A.M.

_____

_____

8. 2 h 25 min after 2:45.

9. 4 h 15 min after 10:15 P.M.

_____

_____

Tell what time it was:

10. 2 h 15 min before 8:45. _____

11. 1 h 30 min before 11:00. _____

12. 4 h before 9:00 A.M. _____

13. 6 hours before 3:00 P.M. _____

14. 3 h 20 min before 6:00. _____

15. 2 h 55 min before 6 P.M. _____

16. Kimi went to a movie that started at 7:30 P.M. The movie lasted 2 hours and 15 minutes. What time did the movie end?

_____

McGraw-Hill School Division

PROBLEM-SOLVING STRATEGY: WORK BACKWARD

✔ **Read**
✔ **Plan**
✔ **Solve**
✔ **Look Back**

Solve by working backward. Use the schedule for problems 1–4.

1. It takes Kumar about 25 minutes to walk to the baseball field. What time does he have to leave home for batting practice?

_____

2. It takes Rico 10 minutes to get to the baseball field. If he wants to arrive at the game a half hour early, when should he leave?

_____

Team Schedule

Monday: batting practice 3:30-4:45

Wednesday: regular practice 4:00-5:30

Saturday: Game - Rockets 10:00

3. Kim is meeting Lee at 1:00 P.M. for ice cream after the game. If it takes Kim 5 minutes to walk to Lee's, what time should she

leave? _____

4. Alex practices batting on Monday. He has to be home by 4:30. It takes him 20 minutes to walk home. How long could he

practice? _____

Solve using any method.
Use the schedule above for problems 5 and 8.

5. How much time altogether could the players spend at practice on Monday and Wednesday?

_____

6. One Saturday game started at 9:10 and ended at 11:00. How long was that game?

_____

7. The team has saved $32 toward new uniforms. They just collected another $15. New uniforms will cost about $85. About how much more do they need?

_____

8. Jacy must spend about 1 hour and 20 minutes doing chores before the game. It takes him about 15 minutes to get to the ball field. When should he begin his chores?

_____

McGraw-Hill School Division

RANGE, MEDIAN, AND MODE

Find the range, median, and mode for the set of data.

1. Numbers of items in students' backpacks:
8, 4, 3, 12, 0, 5, 8

_____

2. Prices of T-shirts:
$9, $13, $23, $15, $14, $13, $13

_____

3. Number of hours a week spent helping at home:
7, 5, 11, 5, 1, 5, 4

_____

4. Number of hours a week spent outside:
24, 9, 8, 21, 7, 8, 11

_____

Use the data in exercises 1–4 above to tell whether the answer is true or false. Then explain your answer.

5. Most students carry more than 8 items in their backpacks.

_____

6. Most students pay $13 for T-shirts. _____

7. Most students help at home for 5 hours. _____

8. The greatest amount of time spent outside is 5 hours

longer than the least amount. _____

9. The greatest number of items carried in backpacks is 12

more than the least number. _____

Solve.

10. Use the data from exercise 4. Add 14 and 18 as data for 2 more people. How does the range, median, or mode change?

_____

PICTOGRAPHS

Use the table and the pictograph for problems 1–4.

1. Dan made a survey. Complete the table and the pictograph to show his results. Which item would the most people miss?

_____

2. How many people were surveyed?

_____

3. How many more people would miss their televisions than their computers?

_____

4. What if Dan surveys 80 people? How could Dan show the data in a pictograph?

_____

WHICH MODERN INVENTION WOULD YOU MISS?

Invention	Tally	Total
Television	卌 III	
Tape Deck	III	
Car	卌	
Computer	II	

Television	🯅 🯅 🯅 🯅
Tape Deck	🯅 🯅
Car	🯅 🯅 🯅
Computer	🯅
Key:	🯅 = 2 people

Use the tables to make pictographs.

5. FAVORITE LUNCHES

Lunch	Tally
Pizza	卌 IIII
Grilled Cheese	卌 I
Spaghetti	卌
Chicken Sandwich	IIII

6. AFTER-LUNCH ACTIVITIES

Activity	Frequency
Drawing	3
Story Listening	24
Doing Homework	9

BAR GRAPHS

Use the line plot for problems 1–3.

1. How many students were at the recreation center on Monday?

_____

2. On which day were there the most students?

_____

3. On which days were there the same number of students?

_____

**Number of Students
at the Recreation Center**

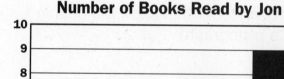

	X
Monday	Tuesday Wednesday Thursday Friday

Number of Students

Monday   Tuesday   Wednesday   Thursday   Friday

Day

Use the bar graph for problems 4–6.

4. During which week did Jon read the greatest number of books?

_____

5. How many books did Jon read in Week 1?

_____

6. Did Jon read more or fewer books in Week 3 than in Week 1? How many more or fewer?

_____

7. What if Jon reads for a fifth week? About how many books do you think Jon might read in Week 5?

_____

Number of Books Read by Jon

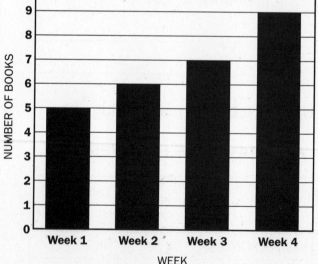

NUMBER OF BOOKS

Week 1   Week 2   Week 3   Week 4

WEEK

ORDERED PAIRS

Hill, Jill, Will, and Gill are playing golf. Write the name of the player at each location.

1. (1,5) _____ **2.** (4,2) _____ **3.** (1,10) _____ **4.** (9,2) _____

The friends play past different objects. Write the ordered pair for the location of each object.

5. cow _____ **6.** birdhouse _____ **7.** windmill _____

8. sunflower _____ **9.** rooster _____ **10.** tunnel _____

11. waterfall _____ **12.** bridge _____ **13.** mountain _____

Solve. Use the grid of the golf course above.

14. The owners of the course decide to add a 10th bonus hole 3 spaces down from the sunflower. What ordered pair names this location?

_____

15. On her second shot, Jill is between the waterfall and her original position. What ordered pair names her new location on the grid?

_____

LINE GRAPHS

Use the line graph for problems 1–4.

1. In which hour were the most people in the card store? How many people were there?

   _____

2. In which hours were there the fewest people in the card store?

   _____

3. How many people were in the card store between 8 and 9 A.M.?

   _____

4. Between which two periods was there the greatest increase in the number of people in the card store?

   _____

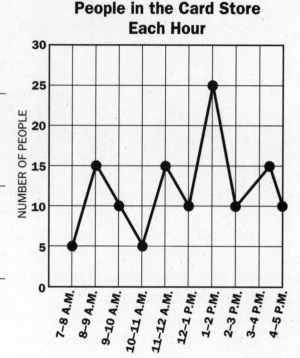

People in the Card Store Each Hour

Use the table for problems 5–8.

5. Make a line graph from the data given.

   _____

6. Between which two days was there the greatest increase in the number of pizzas sold?

   _____

7. Between which two days was there the greatest decrease in the number of pizzas sold?

   _____

PIZZAS SOLD EACH DAY							
Day	M	T	W	T	F	S	S
Number Sold	9	6	14	18	20	19	12

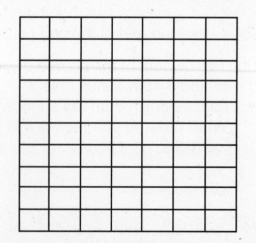

PROBLEM SOLVING: INTERPRET DATA

Solve.

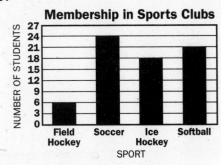

Membership in Sports Clubs

Field Hockey Membership

1. Which sports club has the greatest number of members? How many members?

2. When did membership in field hockey increase the most? By how much did it increase?

3. If 3 students switch from the softball club to the soccer club, how many students will be in the soccer club? the softball club?

4. **What if** five students join the field hockey club each month beginning in April. When will the club reach 25 members?

Solve using any method.

5. Tim spends about a half hour a day practicing trumpet. About how much time does he spend practicing each week?

6. Tim takes trumpet lessons once a week. Each lesson costs $12. About how much do his lessons cost each month?

7. Tim travels 20 minutes to the music store. He is there 30 minutes and then goes home. If he left home at 3:15 P.M., when will he return?

8. Tim buys music for $5, and pays for 2 lessons at $12 each. How much does he spend in all at the music store?

MEANING OF MULTIPLICATION

Write a multiplication sentence for each picture.

1. ⊙⊙⊙⊙
   ⊙⊙⊙⊙

   _____

2. ⊙⊙⊙⊙
   ⊙⊙⊙⊙
   ⊙⊙⊙⊙
   ⊙⊙⊙⊙
   ⊙⊙⊙⊙
   ⊙⊙⊙⊙

   _____

3. ⊙⊙⊙⊙
   ⊙⊙⊙⊙
   ⊙⊙⊙⊙
   ⊙⊙⊙⊙

   _____

4. ⊙⊙⊙⊙
   ⊙⊙⊙⊙

   _____

Multiply using any method.

5. $3 \times 5 =$ _____ 6. $4 \times 6 =$ _____ 7. $0 \times 4 =$ _____ 8. $8 \times 5 =$ _____

9. $7 \times 4 =$ _____ 10. $3 \times 4 =$ _____ 11. $3 \times 7 =$ _____ 12. $5 \times 7 =$ _____

13. $8 \times 2 =$ _____ 14. $7 \times 2 =$ _____ 15. $6 \times 3 =$ _____ 16. $5 \times 6 =$ _____

17. $\begin{array}{r} 4 \\ \times 3 \\ \hline \end{array}$
18. $\begin{array}{r} 1 \\ \times 7 \\ \hline \end{array}$
19. $\begin{array}{r} 8 \\ \times 7 \\ \hline \end{array}$
20. $\begin{array}{r} 0 \\ \times 6 \\ \hline \end{array}$
21. $\begin{array}{r} 9 \\ \times 7 \\ \hline \end{array}$
22. $\begin{array}{r} 5 \\ \times 5 \\ \hline \end{array}$

23. $\begin{array}{r} 4 \\ \times 9 \\ \hline \end{array}$
24. $\begin{array}{r} 9 \\ \times 0 \\ \hline \end{array}$
25. $\begin{array}{r} 5 \\ \times 4 \\ \hline \end{array}$
26. $\begin{array}{r} 4 \\ \times 7 \\ \hline \end{array}$
27. $\begin{array}{r} 3 \\ \times 2 \\ \hline \end{array}$
28. $\begin{array}{r} 7 \\ \times 8 \\ \hline \end{array}$

Solve.

29. Frank is making 5 guitars. Each guitar will have 6 strings. How many strings does Frank need?

   _____

30. Lanie is buying recorders for 3 friends. Each recorder costs $6. How much money does she need?

   _____

McGraw-Hill School Division

MENTAL MATH: 2 THROUGH 5 AS FACTORS

Write a multiplication sentence for each picture.

1. ⊙⊙
   ⊙⊙
   ⊙⊙

_____

2. ⊙⊙
   ⊙⊙
   ⊙⊙
   ⊙⊙

_____

3. ⊙⊙⊙⊙
   ⊙⊙⊙⊙

_____

4. ⊙⊙⊙
   ⊙⊙⊙
   ⊙⊙⊙
   ⊙⊙⊙

_____

Multiply using any method.

5. $2 \times 3 =$ _____   **6.** $4 \times 9 =$ _____   **7.** $5 \times 7 =$ _____   **8.** $3 \times 6 =$ _____

9. $4 \times 5 =$ _____   **10.** $3 \times 8 =$ _____   **11.** $5 \times 2 =$ _____   **12.** $2 \times 9 =$ _____

13. $2 \times 7 =$ _____   **14.** $3 \times 4 =$ _____   **15.** $5 \times 9 =$ _____   **16.** $5 \times 5 =$ _____

17. $\begin{array}{r} 8 \\ \times 5 \\ \hline \end{array}$ **18.** $\begin{array}{r} 9 \\ \times 3 \\ \hline \end{array}$ **19.** $\begin{array}{r} 6 \\ \times 4 \\ \hline \end{array}$ **20.** $\begin{array}{r} 8 \\ \times 2 \\ \hline \end{array}$ **21.** $\begin{array}{r} 5 \\ \times 3 \\ \hline \end{array}$ **22.** $\begin{array}{r} 3 \\ \times 4 \\ \hline \end{array}$

Solve.

23. Tim and Cam play basketball games up to 6 points. Tim won 3 games. Write a number sentence to show how many points Tim scored.

_____

24. In basketball, most baskets made count as 2 points. How many points do you get if you make 7 baskets at 2 points each?

_____

MENTAL MATH:
6 AND 8 AS FACTORS

Multiply using any method.

1. $3 \times 6 =$ _____ **2.** $4 \times 6 =$ _____ **3.** $5 \times 6 =$ _____ **4.** $7 \times 8 =$ _____

5. $8 \times 7 =$ _____ **6.** $9 \times 6 =$ _____ **7.** $6 \times 9 =$ _____ **8.** $0 \times 8 =$ _____

9. $\begin{array}{r} 8 \\ \times\, 5 \\ \hline \end{array}$ **10.** $\begin{array}{r} 1 \\ \times\, 8 \\ \hline \end{array}$ **11.** $\begin{array}{r} 6 \\ \times\, 4 \\ \hline \end{array}$ **12.** $\begin{array}{r} 6 \\ \times\, 6 \\ \hline \end{array}$ **13.** $\begin{array}{r} 2 \\ \times\, 6 \\ \hline \end{array}$

14. $\begin{array}{r} 3 \\ \times\, 8 \\ \hline \end{array}$ **15.** $\begin{array}{r} 7 \\ \times\, 6 \\ \hline \end{array}$ **16.** $\begin{array}{r} 6 \\ \times\, 8 \\ \hline \end{array}$ **17.** $\begin{array}{r} 8 \\ \times\, 2 \\ \hline \end{array}$ **18.** $\begin{array}{r} 6 \\ \times\, 0 \\ \hline \end{array}$

Algebra Complete the multiplication sentence.

19. $\square \times 2 = 12$ **20.** $6 \times \square = 18$ **21.** $8 \times \square = 0$ **22.** $3 \times \square = 24$

23. $\square \times 6 = 12$ **24.** $8 \times \square = 72$ **25.** $3 \times \square = 18$ **26.** $8 \times \square = 40$

27. $8 \times 2 = \square \times 8$ **28.** $8 \times 1 = 1 \times \square$

29. $2 \times 9 = \square \times 6$ **30.** $4 \times 5 = 5 \times \square$

31. $6 \times 8 = (3 \times 8) + (3 \times \square)$ **32.** $8 \times 3 = (4 \times 3) + (\square \times 3)$

33. $9 \times 6 = (3 \times \square) + (3 \times 9)$ **34.** $6 \times 6 = (9 \times 2) + (9 \times \square)$

35. $8 \times 5 = (4 \times 5) + (4 \times \square)$ **36.** $8 \times 2 = (4 \times \square) + (4 \times 2)$

Solve.

37. Each roller hockey team has 5 players. Six teams are in a tournament. How many people are playing?

38. Seven groups of 8 roller hockey players practice passing the puck. How many players are practicing?

_____   _____

McGraw-Hill School Division

MENTAL MATH:
7 AND 9 AS FACTORS

Multiply mentally.

1. $7 \times 4 =$ _____   **2.** $4 \times 9 =$ _____   **3.** $7 \times 3 =$ _____   **4.** $3 \times 9 =$ _____

5. $9 \times 2 =$ _____   **6.** $5 \times 7 =$ _____   **7.** $7 \times 5 =$ _____   **8.** $9 \times 1 =$ _____

9. 9
$\times 6$

10. 7
$\times 1$

11. 8
$\times 9$

12. 7
$\times 0$

13. 8
$\times 7$

14. 9
$\times 5$

15. 6
$\times 9$

16. 0
$\times 9$

17. 5
$\times 9$

18. 2
$\times 7$

You can choose one factor from each box. Show at least two ways to get the product.

19. 8 _____

20. 10 _____

21. 16 _____

22. 20 _____

23. 45 _____

24. 63 _____

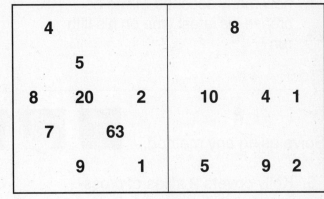

4			8		
5					
8	20	2	10	4	1
7	63				
9	1		5	9	2

Solve.

25. There are 6 players on a team in ice hockey. In one tournament there are 7 ice hockey teams. How many players is that?

_____

26. The tournament committee wants to give each team 9 official shirts. There are 8 teams in the tournament. How many shirts should they buy?

_____

PROBLEM-SOLVING STRATEGY: FIND A PATTERN

Solve by finding a pattern.

1. Kevin runs 20 minutes every day. He increases his time by 5 minutes every week. At the end of the fifth week, how many minutes does he run each day?

_____

2. Kevin runs 8 miles his first week, 10 miles his third, and 12 miles his fifth. If he increases his distance at this rate, how many miles will he run his eleventh week?

_____

3. On his second run, Jack decreased his time by 10 seconds. On his third run, he decreased his latest time by 7 seconds. On his fourth run, he decreased his latest time by 4 seconds. At this rate, by how many seconds will he decrease his latest time on his fifth run?

_____

4. Eighteen students entered the first triathalon. Twenty-two students entered the second triathalon, and 26 entered the third. If the pattern continues, how many students will enter the fifth triathalon?

_____

Solve using any method.

5. Kelly covers 2 miles of cross-country ski trails every Saturday. How many miles does she cover in 9 Saturdays?

_____

6. There are 6 inches of snow at the beginning of a storm. Snow piles up at a rate of 2 inches every hour. How much snow will there be after 6 hours?

_____

7. Jon skis 21 hours each week. If he skis the same number of hours each day, how many hours does he ski per day?

_____

8. The ski lift goes up and down the mountain once every 5 minutes. How many times will it go up and down the mountain in 45 minutes?

_____

Grade 4, Chapter 4, Lesson 5, pages 138–139

THREE FACTORS

Multiply.

1. $4 \times (2 \times 5) =$ _____   **2.** $4 \times (2 \times 3) =$ _____   **3.** $7 \times (2 \times 5) =$ _____

4. $(3 \times 2) \times 8 =$ _____   **5.** $(4 \times 3) \times 2 =$ _____   **6.** $6 \times (3 \times 2) =$ _____

7. $4 \times (4 \times 2) =$ _____   **8.** $(2 \times 2) \times 2 =$ _____   **9.** $(3 \times 0) \times 9 =$ _____

10. $(5 \times 2) \times 4 =$ _____   **11.** $8 \times (2 \times 2) =$ _____   **12.** $7 \times (3 \times 3) =$ _____

13. $6 \times (2 \times 2) =$ _____   **14.** $(2 \times 7) \times 2 =$ _____   **15.** $(4 \times 3) \times 0 =$ _____

16. $5 \times (4 \times 2) =$ _____   **17.** $9 \times (2 \times 4) =$ _____   **18.** $5 \times (3 \times 3) =$ _____

19. $4 \times (6 \times 1) =$ _____   **20.** $2 \times (5 \times 0) =$ _____   **21.** $7 \times (3 \times 2) =$ _____

22. $9 \times (2 \times 3) =$ _____   **23.** $(8 \times 1) \times 9 =$ _____   **24.** $5 \times (2 \times 3) =$ _____

Algebra Complete the multiplication sentence.

25. $5 \times 6 = 5 \times (3 \times \boxed{})$ **26.** $3 \times (5 \times \boxed{}) = 60$

27. $(\boxed{} \times 8) \times 7 = 0$ **28.** $9 \times (\boxed{} \times 1) = 27$

29. $(2 \times 4) \times \boxed{} = 24$ **30.** $(3 \times 5) \times \boxed{} = 9 \times 5$

31. $3 \times 6 = 3 \times (3 \times \boxed{})$ **32.** $3 \times 8 = 3 \times (2 \times \boxed{})$

33. $3 \times 16 = 3 \times (4 \times \boxed{})$ **34.** $4 \times 6 = (3 \times 4) \times \boxed{}$

Solve.

35. The school gives each tennis player a blue shirt and a white shirt. Each shirt costs the school $9. What is the total cost of shirts for 5 players?

36. Two cans of tennis balls are needed for each tennis match. There are 3 tennis balls in each can. How many balls are needed for 5 matches?

_____   _____

McGraw-Hill School Division

MEANING OF DIVISION

Complete the division sentence for the picture. Write whether you divided to find the *number of groups* or the *number in each group.*

1. 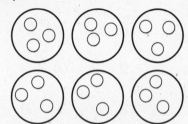 **2.**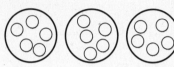

$18 \div 3 =$ _____ $15 \div 5 =$ _____

3. 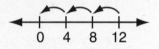 **4.**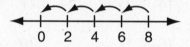

$12 \div 3 =$ _____ $8 \div 2 =$ _____

Divide using any method.

5. $16 \div 4 =$ _____   **6.** $27 \div 3 =$ _____   **7.** $18 \div 9 =$ _____

8. $20 \div 4 =$ _____   **9.** $24 \div 6 =$ _____   **10.** $28 \div 7 =$ _____

11. $14 \div 2 =$ _____   **12.** $54 \div 6 =$ _____

13. $5\overline{)25}$ **14.** $1\overline{)6}$ **15.** $4\overline{)28}$ **16.** $9\overline{)81}$

Algebra Write the missing number.

17. $48 \div 6 =$ _____   **18.** $27 \div 3 =$ _____   **19.** $21 \div$ _____ $= 3$

20. _____ $\div 4 = 9$ **21.** _____ $\div 6 = 3$ **22.** _____ $\div 7 = 6$

23. _____ $\div 5 = 5$ **24.** $9 \div$ _____ $= 3$ **25.** $35 \div$ _____ $= 5$

26. $8 \div 4 =$ _____ $\times 2$ **27.** $3 \times$ _____ $= 12 \div 2$ **28.** $27 \div$ _____ $= 63 \div 7$

McGraw-Hill School Division

Name: _____

2 THROUGH 5 AS DIVISORS

Write a division sentence for each picture.

1. ○○○○○
    ○○○○○

2. ○○○○○○
    ○○○○○○
    ○○○○○○

3. ○○○○○○○○○○
    ○○○○○○○○○○
    ○○○○○○○○○○

_____   _____   _____

Divide.

4. $35 \div 5 =$ _____   **5.** $28 \div 4 =$ _____   **6.** $12 \div 2 =$ _____

7. $45 \div 5 =$ _____   **8.** $18 \div 2 =$ _____   **9.** $12 \div 3 =$ _____

10. $32 \div 4 =$ _____   **11.** $24 \div 3 =$ _____   **12.** $40 \div 5 =$ _____

13. $0 \div 2 =$ _____   **14.** $15 \div 3 =$ _____   **15.** $18 \div 3 =$ _____

16. $2\overline{)10}$ **17.** $3\overline{)15}$ **18.** $5\overline{)20}$ **19.** $4\overline{)12}$ **20.** $1\overline{)5}$

21. $4\overline{)16}$ **22.** $5\overline{)25}$ **23.** $3\overline{)24}$ **24.** $4\overline{)32}$ **25.** $3\overline{)27}$

26. $5\overline{)40}$ **27.** $4\overline{)12}$ **28.** $5\overline{)45}$ **29.** $4\overline{)36}$ **30.** $5\overline{)40}$

Algebra Find the missing factor.

31. $3 \times \square = 24$ **32.** $4 \times \square = 24$ **33.** $\square \times 5 = 45$ **34.** $\square \times 3 = 15$

Solve.

35. There are 4 runners on each team in a relay race. How many teams can be formed from 16 runners?

36. Each relay team needs 4 shirts. The coach has 28 school shirts. How many teams are there enough shirts for?

_____   _____

McGraw-Hill School Division

6 THROUGH 9 AS DIVISORS

Write a division sentence for each picture.

1.

2.

3.

_____   _____   _____

Divide.

4. $54 \div 9 =$ _____   **5.** $35 \div 7 =$ _____   **6.** $0 \div 7 =$ _____

7. $36 \div 9 =$ _____   **8.** $63 \div 9 =$ _____   **9.** $6 \div 6 =$ _____

10. $42 \div 6 =$ _____   **11.** $48 \div 8 =$ _____   **12.** $72 \div 8 =$ _____

13. $64 \div 8 =$ _____   **14.** $9 \div 9 =$ _____   **15.** $0 \div 8 =$ _____

16. $7\overline{)28}$ **17.** $6\overline{)24}$ **18.** $6\overline{)18}$ **19.** $8\overline{)64}$ **20.** $7\overline{)49}$

21. $6\overline{)36}$ **22.** $9\overline{)27}$ **23.** $9\overline{)81}$ **24.** $6\overline{)54}$ **25.** $9\overline{)72}$

Algebra Find the missing factor.

26. $7 \times \boxed{} = 28$ **27.** $9 \times \boxed{} = 81$ **28.** $8 \times \boxed{} = 40$ **29.** $\boxed{} \times 6 = 30$

30. $5 \times \boxed{} = 30$ **31.** $3 \times \boxed{} = 21$ **32.** $2 \times \boxed{} = 18$ **33.** $\boxed{} \times 7 = 35$

Solve.

34. There are 54 students in all of the fourth grade classes. How many baseball teams can you form with 9 players on each team?

35. Pete's swim team has 24 members. One school van can take 8 swimmers to the swim meet. How many vans are needed?

_____   _____

FACT FAMILIES

Write the fact family for the set of numbers.

1. 4, 3, 12   **2.** 8, 3, 24   **3.** 6, 4, 24   **4.** 5, 9, 45

_____   _____   _____   _____

_____   _____   _____   _____

_____   _____   _____   _____

_____   _____   _____   _____

5. 7, 5, 35   **6.** 7, 3, 21   **7.** 7, 9, 63   **8.** 5, 8, 40

_____   _____   _____   _____

_____   _____   _____   _____

_____   _____   _____   _____

_____   _____   _____   _____

Algebra Find the missing number. Use the related sentence at the right to solve. Draw a line to show the related sentence.

9. $28 \div \boxed{} = 4$ **a.** $16 \div 4 = 4$

10. $4 \times \boxed{} = 16$ **b.** $42 \div 6 = 7$

11. $\boxed{} \div 9 = 3$ **c.** $4 \times 7 = 28$

12. $6 \times \boxed{} = 42$ **d.** $3 \times 9 = 27$

Solve.

13. Karim wants to put up 9 posters on each floor of the school. The school has 4 floors. How many posters will he need?

_____

14. Tickets to the school play cost $3. Joanna spent $21. How many tickets did she buy?

_____

REMAINDERS

Divide.

1. $19 \div 6 =$ _____   **2.** $15 \div 6 =$ _____   **3.** $22 \div 7 =$ _____

4. $29 \div 4 =$ _____   **5.** $53 \div 7 =$ _____   **6.** $44 \div 5 =$ _____

7. $39 \div 4 =$ _____   **8.** $36 \div 8 =$ _____   **9.** $19 \div 5 =$ _____

10. $62 \div 7 =$ _____   **11.** $25 \div 8 =$ _____   **12.** $80 \div 9 =$ _____

13. $6\overline{)57}$ **14.** $8\overline{)69}$ **15.** $5\overline{)31}$ **16.** $5\overline{)48}$ **17.** $8\overline{)29}$

18. $7\overline{)65}$ **19.** $9\overline{)32}$ **20.** $5\overline{)27}$ **21.** $6\overline{)27}$ **22.** $6\overline{)39}$

23. $8\overline{)64}$ **24.** $5\overline{)29}$ **25.** $8\overline{)48}$ **26.** $7\overline{)33}$ **27.** $9\overline{)66}$

28. $7\overline{)49}$ **29.** $6\overline{)58}$ **30.** $5\overline{)49}$ **31.** $3\overline{)28}$ **32.** $8\overline{)63}$

Solve.

33. After the tennis match, Kim found 14 tennis balls. She has cans that hold 3 balls in each. How many full cans will she have? how many extra balls?

34. The baseball team brings 26 baseball bats to the game. Each bag holds 8 bats. How many bags are loaded onto the bus?

_____

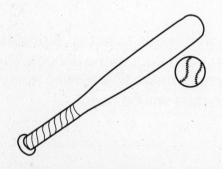

McGraw-Hill School Division

PROBLEM SOLVING: CHOOSE THE OPERATION

✔ Read
✔ Plan
✔ Solve
✔ Look Back

Solve. Tell which operation you used.

1. There are 3 softball teams. There are 9 students on each team. How many students play softball?

_____

2. Tyrone forms 4 teams for a relay race. There are 24 students. How many students will there be on each team?

_____

3. Ellen ran the first leg of a 4-leg relay race in 3 minutes. If the others on her team run just as fast, about how long will it take the team to finish the race?

_____

4. The students started playing a softball game at 1:20 P.M. The game lasted 1 hour and 50 minutes. What time did the game end?

_____

Solve using any method.

5. A standard soccer field is 100 yards long and 50 yards wide. On a scale drawing, 1 inch represents 10 yards. How long is the field on the scale drawing?

_____

6. It takes Veronica 25 minutes to get to soccer practice. If practice starts at 4:00, what time should she leave home? On Friday, she needs an extra 15 minutes before practice to buy socks. What time should she leave home on Friday?

_____

7. Veronica has soccer practice for 2 hours 3 times a week. How many hours does she practice in 4 weeks?

_____

8. Logical Reasoning The fourth grade chooses sides for kickball by counting off "1, 2, 1, 2. . ." Will the 29th student be on the 1s' team or the 2s' team?

_____

MENTAL MATH: MULTIPLICATION PATTERNS

Multiply mentally.

1. $2 \times 100 =$ _____   2. $2 \times 600 =$ _____   3. $2 \times 3,000 =$ _____

4. $2 \times 30 =$ _____   5. $4,000 \times 2 =$ _____   6. $20 \times 3 =$ _____

7. $40 \times 3 =$ _____   8. $30 \times 7 =$ _____   9. $3 \times 7,000 =$ _____

10. $3,000 \times 7 =$ _____   11. $300 \times 2 =$ _____   12. $800 \times 5 =$ _____

13. $200 \times 4 =$ _____   14. $8 \times 5,000 =$ _____   15. $5 \times 400 =$ _____

16. $6 \times 8,000 =$ _____   17. $3 \times 600 =$ _____   18. $6 \times 5,000 =$ _____

19. $7 \times 600 =$ _____   20. $5,000 \times 7 =$ _____   21. $9 \times 200 =$ _____

22. $9,000 \times 4 =$ _____   23. $6,000 \times 4 =$ _____   24. $6 \times 700 =$ _____

Algebra Find the missing number.

25. $5 \times$ _____ $= 450$ 26. $8 \times$ _____ $= 1,600$

27. _____ $\times 9 = 2,700$ 28. _____ $\times 6 = 18,000$

29. $4 \times$ _____ $= 28,000$ 30. _____ $\times 30 = 180$

Solve.

31. At 8 A.M., each of LMO Limousine Company's 40 vans was carrying 7 passengers. How many passengers were in LMO vans at 8 A.M.?

32. There were 2,000 people who rode LMO vans yesterday. Each person bought a ticket for $8. How much money did LMO take in yesterday?

_____   _____

McGraw-Hill School Division

MENTAL MATH: ESTIMATING PRODUCTS

Estimate the product.

1. $8 \times 67 =$ _____   **2.** $4 \times 54 =$ _____

3. $2 \times 94 =$ _____   **4.** $7 \times \$21 =$ _____

5. $9 \times 738 =$ _____   **6.** $811 \times 3 =$ _____

7. $5 \times \$517 =$ _____   **8.** $6 \times 973 =$ _____

9. $3 \times 6,712 =$ _____   **10.** $9 \times 8,210 =$ _____

11. $\$4,821 \times 7 =$ _____   **12.** $4,189 \times 9 =$ _____

| **13.** $\begin{array}{r} 6,450 \\ \times\quad 3 \\ \hline \end{array}$ | **14.** $\begin{array}{r} 6,237 \\ \times\quad 9 \\ \hline \end{array}$ | **15.** $\begin{array}{r} \$9,513 \\ \times\quad 5 \\ \hline \end{array}$ | **16.** $\begin{array}{r} 2,686 \\ \times\quad 6 \\ \hline \end{array}$ | **17.** $\begin{array}{r} 1,931 \\ \times\quad 2 \\ \hline \end{array}$ |

| **18.** $\begin{array}{r} 3,722 \\ \times\quad 4 \\ \hline \end{array}$ | **19.** $\begin{array}{r} 7,745 \\ \times\quad 8 \\ \hline \end{array}$ | **20.** $\begin{array}{r} 4,376 \\ \times\quad 7 \\ \hline \end{array}$ | **21.** $\begin{array}{r} 3,894 \\ \times\quad 2 \\ \hline \end{array}$ | **22.** $\begin{array}{r} 5,618 \\ \times\quad 6 \\ \hline \end{array}$ |

Algebra Estimate. Write > or <.

23. $5 \times 446 \bigcirc 1,950$ **24.** $6,092 \times 7 \bigcirc 52,100$ **25.** $4,399 \bigcirc 6 \times 888$

26. $8 \times 675 \bigcirc 4,800$ **27.** $7,310 \times 9 \bigcirc 63,100$ **28.** $4 \times 6,498 \bigcirc 28,150$

29. A bike club is ordering 6 repair kits. Each kit costs $27. About how much will it cost to order the kits?

30. A bicycle tire makes about 776 rotations in a mile. About how many rotations will the tire make in 8 miles?

_____   _____

USING MODELS TO MULTIPLY

Find the total number of squares in the rectangle without counting.

1.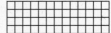

_____

2.

_____

3.

_____

4.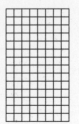

_____

5.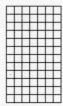

_____

6.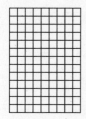

_____

Find the product using any method.

7. $5 \times 20 =$ _____

8. $6 \times 31 =$ _____

9. $4 \times 22 =$ _____

10. $3 \times 28 =$ _____

11. $8 \times 17 =$ _____

12. $3 \times 74 =$ _____

13. $\begin{array}{r} 43 \\ \times\ 5 \\ \hline \end{array}$

14. $\begin{array}{r} 37 \\ \times\ 2 \\ \hline \end{array}$

15. $\begin{array}{r} 60 \\ \times\ 3 \\ \hline \end{array}$

16. $\begin{array}{r} 55 \\ \times\ 6 \\ \hline \end{array}$

Solve.

17. Tina's bedroom floor is a rectangle. It has 9 square tiles along the front and 15 along the side. How many square tiles cover her floor?

_____

18. Vernon's bedroom floor has 12 square tiles along the front and 8 square tiles along the side. How many square tiles cover his floor?

_____

MULTIPLYING 2-DIGIT NUMBERS

Find only the products that are greater than 300.
Use estimation to help you decide.

| 1. 42 $\times$ 6 | 2. 53 $\times$ 7 | 3. 51 $\times$ 4 | 4. 48 $\times$ 8 | 5. 65 $\times$ 9 |

| 6. 14 $\times$ 5 | 7. 76 $\times$ 8 | 8. 88 $\times$ 4 | 9. 91 $\times$ 3 | 10. 37 $\times$ 9 |

| 11. 42 $\times$ 9 | 12. 45 $\times$ 5 | 13. 74 $\times$ 8 | 14. 88 $\times$ 2 | 15. 59 $\times$ 9 |

| 16. 63 $\times$ 8 | 17. 37 $\times$ 6 | 18. 58 $\times$ 6 | 19. 96 $\times$ 4 | 20. 85 $\times$ 9 |

21. $5 \times 87 =$ _____   22. $74 \times 6 =$ _____   23. $6 \times 93 =$ _____

24. $8 \times 63 =$ _____   25. $9 \times 57 =$ _____   26. $4 \times 28 =$ _____

27. $56 \times 7 =$ _____   28. $9 \times 18 =$ _____   29. $7 \times 96 =$ _____

Algebra Find the missing digit.

| 30. 23 $\times \square$ ——— 92 | 31. $\square$8 $\times$ 6 ——— 348 | 32. 4$\square$ $\times$ 5 ——— 235 | 33. $\square$7 $\times \square$ ——— 74 |

Solve.

34. Buses from Tours, Inc. hold 54 passengers. How many passengers will 6 of these buses hold?

35. A bus traveled at a speed of 55 miles per hour for 3 hours. How many miles did it travel in that time?

_____   _____

PROBLEM-SOLVING STRATEGY: SOLVE MULTISTEP PROBLEMS

✔ Read
✔ Plan
✔ Solve
✔ Look Back

Solve.

1. It is 22 miles between Ms. Castro's home and her office. She drives to and from work 5 days a week. How many miles does she drive getting to and from work each week?

   _____

2. Ms. Cata earns $9 an hour. She works 35 hours each week. She sets aside $70 a week to pay for rent. How much does she have left a week to spend?

   _____

3. Mr. Schwab works 22 hours a week at one job, earning $8 an hour. He works 16 hours a week at another job, earning $6 an hour. How much does he earn altogether each week?

   _____

4. During 4 weeks in May, Jesse put $29 a week in his savings account. He already had $378 in his account. How much does he have at the end of May?

   _____

Solve using any strategy.

5. Becky needs to leave at 3 P.M. She began painting at 9:00 A.M. How many hours can she paint?

   _____

6. Ann sold 172 dolls for $8 each. How much money did she make?

   _____

7. Ann sewed buttons on the three dolls she made today. She sewed 6 buttons on one doll, 5 buttons on another doll, and 4 buttons on a third doll. At the end of the day, she had 14 buttons left. How many did she start out with?

   _____

8. **Logical Reasoning** Alex, Betty, and Cara make crafts. One paints, another knits, and the third carves wood. Alex does not work with wood. Betty likes to knit. Cara does not knit. Who does what?

   _____

MULTIPLYING GREATER NUMBERS

Multiply. Remember to estimate.

1.	210 × 6	2.	192 × 6	3.	482 × 2	4.	$608 × 5	5.	971 × 4

6.	1,921 × 7	7.	3,922 × 8	8.	8,694 × 5	9.	7,165 × 6	10.	$4,377 × 7

11.	1,396 × 3	12.	7,408 × 9	13.	$5,129 × 5	14.	$8,888 × 2	15.	6,534 × 7

16. $6 \times 666 =$ _____ **17.** $4 \times 4{,}793 =$ _____ **18.** $7 \times \$6{,}660 =$ _____

19. $5 \times 283 =$ _____ **20.** $9 \times 342 =$ _____ **21.** $3 \times 862 =$ _____

22. Find the product of 5 and $379. _____

23. What is 4 times 4,321? _____

Algebra Complete the table.

24.

RULE: Multiply by 4.	
Input	**Output**
36	
125	
8,792	

25.

RULE:	
Input	**Output**
43	129
210	630
5,100	15,300

26.

RULE:	
Input	**Output**
51	306
401	2,406
3,002	18,012

MULTIPLYING WITH MONEY

Multiply. Remember to estimate.

1. $0.37
   ×   9

2. $0.68
   ×   3

3. $0.67
   ×   4

4. $0.59
   ×   5

5. $0.71
   ×   6

6. $2.82
   ×   5

7. $7.77
   ×   7

8. $8.57
   ×   2

9. $9.41
   ×   5

10. $6.43
    ×   6

11. $46.75
    ×   8

12. $77.70
    ×   8

13. $12.34
    ×   9

14. $50.89
    ×   8

15. $43.67
    ×   7

16. $38.14
    ×   6

17. $80.72
    ×   3

18. $92.53
    ×   4

19. $71.64
    ×   9

20. $56.85
    ×   5

21. 2 × $0.67 = _____

22. 3 × $5.67 = _____

23. 7 × $2.95 = _____

24. $4.23 × 8 = _____

25. 4 × $92.81 = _____

26. $64.64 × 7 = _____

27. 6 × $71.63 = _____

28. $54.93 × 4 = _____

29. $81.99 × 5 = _____

Solve.

30. A computer costs $1,965. How much would it cost your school to buy 8 computers?

_____

31. A mathematics software program costs $48.95. How much would it cost your school to buy 3 of those software programs?

_____

McGraw-Hill School Division

PROBLEM SOLVING: INTERPRET DATA

Use the pictograph to solve problems 1–4.

98ᵗʰ STREET PET STORE GOLDFISH SALES	
March	🐟 🐟 🐟 🐟
April	🐟 🐟 🐟 🐟 🐟 🐟
May	🐟 🐟
June	🐟 🐟 🐟

🐟 = 25 goldfish   Each goldfish sold for $2.

1. In which month did the pet store sell the least goldfish?

_____

2. In which months were at least $200 worth of goldfish sold?

_____

4. What if the pet store sold 100 goldfish in July. How much money would the store have made in the months March through July?

_____

3. Were more goldfish sold in April, or in May and June combined?

_____

Solve.

5. A pet store sells 4 cans of cat food for $2, 8 cans for $4, and 12 cans for $6. How many cans would you get for $10?

_____

6. Keira has $7 left after going to the pet store. She bought 3 toys for her kitten for $3 each. How much money did she start out with?

_____

7. Pets for You has 48 parakeets. There are twice as many female parakeets as male parakeets. How many parakeets are female? male?

_____

8. Nick buys a fish tank through a TV ad. He makes 3 payments of $39.95 each to pay for it. He also pays $7.50 for shipping. What is the total cost of the fish tank?

_____

MENTAL MATH: MULTIPLICATION PATTERNS

Multiply mentally.

1. $40 \times 10 =$ _____   **2.** $20 \times 80 =$ _____   **3.** $12 \times 10 =$ _____

4. $90 \times 40 =$ _____   **5.** $80 \times 200 =$ _____   **6.** $30 \times 300 =$ _____

7. $30 \times 70 =$ _____   **8.** $50 \times 300 =$ _____   **9.** $80 \times 80 =$ _____

10. $400 \times 30 =$ _____   **11.** $600 \times 20 =$ _____   **12.** $40 \times 1,000 =$ _____

13. $500 \times 20 =$ _____   **14.** $300 \times 80 =$ _____   **15.** $700 \times 90 =$ _____

16. $600 \times 30 =$ _____   **17.** $60 \times 700 =$ _____   **18.** $40 \times 700 =$ _____

19. $800 \times 60 =$ _____   **20.** $600 \times 60 =$ _____   **21.** $5,000 \times 20 =$ _____

Algebra Find the missing number.

22. $200 \times$ _____ $= 8,000$ **23.** _____ $\times 400 = 16,000$

24. $90 \times$ _____ $= 90,000$ **25.** _____ $\times 700 = 21,000$

26. $80 \times$ _____ $= 48,000$ **27.** $500 \times$ _____ $= 25,000$

28. $800 \times$ _____ $= 32,000$ **29.** _____ $\times 90 = 27,000$

30. $30 \times$ _____ $= 24,000$ **31.** $90 \times$ _____ $= 36,000$

Solve.

32. A company puts 30 cans of tennis balls in a box. How many cans are in 200 boxes? in 1,000 boxes?

33. A tennis club uses 5,000 balls in a year. How many does it use in 10 years? in 20 years?

_____

_____

McGraw-Hill School Division

MENTAL MATH: ESTIMATE PRODUCTS

Estimate the product.

1. 31 × 295 _____   **2.** 14 × 68 _____   **3.** 204 × 83 _____

4. 42 × 39 _____   **5.** 586 × 19 _____   **6.** 432 × 25 _____

7. 9,218 × 41 _____   **8.** 3,148 × 36 _____   **9.** $2,325 × 23 _____

10. $23 × 4,607 _____   **11.** 2,482 × 19 _____   **12.** 91 × 7,102 _____

13.	83	**14.**	68	**15.**	$240	**16.**	765	**17.**	349
	× 24		× 32		× 39		× 63		× 52

18.	7,389	**19.**	4,699	**20.**	6,179	**21.**	$2,911	**22.**	$3,701
	× 31		× 67		× 56		× 18		× 93

Estimate. Write > or <.

23. 11 × 21 ◯ 200   **24.** 10 × 50 ◯ 550   **25.** 23 × 19 ◯ 300

26. 42 × 51 ◯ 2,000   **27.** 37 × 194 ◯ 8,000   **28.** 18 × 802 ◯ 16,000

29. 54 × 323 ◯ 15,000   **30.** 76 × 168 ◯ 16,000   **31.** 12 × 877 ◯ 9,000

32. 91 × 9,293 ◯ 810,000   **33.** 8,724 × 26 ◯ 270,000

Solve.

34. A group of 37 students goes to the theater on a class trip. The cost of one ticket is $25. About how much do all the tickets cost?

35. There are 28 performances of the play. The theater holds 565 people. About how many people could see the play?

_____   _____

MULTIPLY 2-DIGIT NUMBERS

Find the total number of squares in the rectangle without counting.

1.
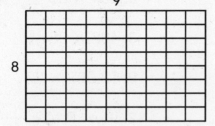

2.
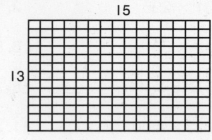

3.
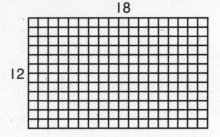

4.
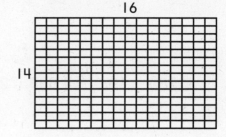

Multiply using any method.

5. 33 × 20	**6.** 12 × 21	**7.** 27 × 17	**8.** 18 × 13	**9.** 15 × 13
10. 18 × 27	**11.** 25 × 11	**12.** 29 × 28	**13.** 14 × 42	**14.** 37 × 22
15. 16 × 27	**16.** 24 × 19	**17.** 35 × 26	**18.** 46 × 32	**19.** 23 × 38
20. 23 × 47	**21.** 42 × 76	**22.** 17 × 25	**23.** 19 × 82	**24.** 93 × 28

Name: _____

Practice 53

MULTIPLY 2-DIGIT NUMBERS

Multiply using any method. Remember to estimate.

1.	2.	3.	4.	5.
14 ×16	18 ×13	23 ×15	34 ×18	37 ×20

6.	7.	8.	9.	10.
27 ×45	30 ×33	42 ×20	57 ×34	82 ×51

11.	12.	13.	14.	15.
76 ×45	63 ×19	$32 ×25	$19 ×18	$30 ×17

16.	17.	18.	19.	20.
$52 ×17	37 ×16	28 ×25	26 ×31	41 ×28

21. $16 \times 40 =$ _____   22. $16 \times 42 =$ _____   23. $37 \times 25 =$ _____

24. $24 \times 87 =$ _____   25. $52 \times 17 =$ _____   26. $46 \times 29 =$ _____

Algebra Ring the letter of the missing number.

27. $50 \times \square = 2,500$ a. 20 b. 50 c. 25 d. 5

28. $\square \times 44 = 1,804$ a. 40 b. 26 c. 62 d. 41

Solve.

29. Sam's Sport Shop sold 23 ski jackets for $48 each. How much money did they make on ski jackets?

30. The sport shop also sold 63 pairs of ski boots for $99 each. How much money did they make on ski boots?

McGraw-Hill School Division

Grade 4, Chapter 6, Lesson 4, pages 214–217   Practice • 53

PROBLEM-SOLVING STRATEGY: USE ALTERNATE SOLUTION METHODS

Solve. Explain your method. What other method could you have used?

1. Sandra's house is the eighth house from the corner. The first house on the corner is number 26 and the numbers go up in order as you move toward Sandra's house. All the houses on her side of the street have even numbers. What is her house number?

_____

2. Jay's street has 10 houses on each side. Each house has room for 2 cars to park in front. How many cars can park on his street at one time?

_____

_____

3. Alfredo's house number is between 20 and 35. The sum of the digits is less than 5. If you subtract 1 from it, you get a multiple of 3. If you add 3 to it, you get a multiple of 5. What is Alfredo's house number?

_____

_____

4. Ed's neighbors empty recycling bins every other week on Monday. Today is the eighth day of the month. Yesterday was recycling day. On which day of the month will they recycle again?

_____

_____

Solve using any strategy.

5. Sandra delivers newspapers in her neighborhood. She delivered the paper every day for 398 days to 11 houses on her street. About how many papers did she deliver?

_____

6. Alfredo cares for cats when their owners are away. He gets $6 per cat per day. Alfredo cared for Sandra's 2 cats for 3 weeks. How much money did he make?

_____

MULTIPLY 3-DIGIT NUMBERS AND MONEY

Multiply. Remember to estimate.

1.	515	**2.**	299	**3.**	895	**4.**	598	**5.**	243
	× 12		× 15		× 18		× 14		× 24

6.	191	**7.**	321	**8.**	275	**9.**	429	**10.**	613
	× 37		× 44		× 13		× 22		× 16

11.	735	**12.**	$4.05	**13.**	$6.39	**14.**	520	**15.**	704
	× 28		× 17		× 32		× 19		× 25

16.	317	**17.**	809	**18.**	$0.68	**19.**	456	**20.**	687
	× 86		× 53		× 48		× 35		× 37

21. 105 × 25 = _____

22. 35 × 491 = _____

23. 28 × $3.99 = _____

24. 16 × 450 = _____

25. 10 × 215 = _____

26. 21 × 313 = _____

27. 25 × 287 = _____

28. 37 × 502 = _____

29. 43 × 629 = _____

30. 28 × $4.97 = _____

31. 53 × 738 = _____

32. 62 × $5.78 = _____

Solve.

33. Dan finds out that he uses 25 gallons of water to take a shower. How many gallons is that a year if Dan takes a shower on 350 days?

34. Dan drinks 1 large bottle of water a day. Each bottle costs $1.29. How much does Dan spend on water in 2 weeks?

_____

_____

MULTIPLY GREATER NUMBERS

Multiply mentally.

1. 3,000 $\times$ 40	**2.** 6,000 $\times$ 20	**3.** 7,000 $\times$ 20	**4.** 5,000 $\times$ 30	**5.** 16,000 $\times$ 20
6. 14,000 $\times$ 50	**7.** 32,000 $\times$ 30	**8.** 28,000 $\times$ 30	**9.** 41,000 $\times$ 20	**10.** 9,000 $\times$ 40

Multiply using any method. Remember to estimate.

11. 254 $\times$ 47	**12.** $6.35 $\times$ 12	**13.** 638 $\times$ 46	**14.** $9.50 $\times$ 26
15. $26.50 $\times$ 32	**16.** $14.95 $\times$ 18	**17.** $32.99 $\times$ 11	**18.** $65.00 $\times$ 12
19. 28.89 $\times$ 9	**20.** $18.99 $\times$ 12	**21.** 3,046 $\times$ 18	**22.** 5,070 $\times$ 96
23. 37,000 $\times$ 64	**24.** 18,200 $\times$ 36	**25.** 23,600 $\times$ 42	**26.** 334,600 $\times$ 28

27. 31 $\times$ 4,650 _____

28. 48 $\times$ 6,600 _____

29. 71 $\times$ $35.50 _____

30. 13 $\times$ $19.88 _____

Solve.

31. A school sells fancy wrapping paper to raise funds. They make $1.15 on each package of paper sold. They sell 435 packages. How much money do they make?

32. The students also rake leaves to raise money. They charge $1.50 a bag. They fill 238 bags. How much money do they make raking leaves?

_____

_____

McGraw-Hill School Division

PROBLEM SOLVING: USE AN ESTIMATE OR FIND THE EXACT ANSWER

✔ Read
✔ Plan
✔ Solve
✔ Look Back

Solve. Tell whether you can use an estimate to solve.

1. Your class puts out a magazine that 178 students buy. Your profit on each magazine is 3¢. How much money have you made?

_____

_____

2. Your class also delivers the magazines. If 129 magazines of the 178 were already delivered, how many more had to be delivered?

_____

_____

3. You have $38 for magazine supplies. You plan to spend $11.95, $23.83, and $19.50. How much more will you need?

_____

_____

4. Caesar's goal is to sell over 300 magazines. Last month he sold 281. Today he sold 33. Has he met his goal?

_____

_____

Solve using any method.

5. Last year, the class put out 2 issues of its magazine each month for 10 months. This year it put out 22 issues. In which year did it put out more issues?

_____

_____

6. Tim wrote an article for the magazine. It started on page 22 and went through page 25. It was continued on pages 57 to 61. How many pages long was his article?

_____

_____

7. Ann makes a pictograph to show 480 magazine readers. The key is one tiny magazine for 20 readers. How many magazines are in her graph?

_____

_____

8. One fourth-grade class of 30 students buys 15 magazines to share in one month. How many do they buy in 8 months?

_____

_____

LENGTH IN CUSTOMARY UNITS

Estimate and then measure.

1. length of your thumb _____

2. length of your longest strand of hair _____

3. width of your math book _____

4. height of your desk _____

5. length of your desk _____

Ring the letter of the best estimate.

6. height of a drinking glass	**a.** 6 in.	**b.** 6 ft	**c.** 6 yd
7. height of a sixth grader	**a.** 5 in.	**b.** 5 ft	**c.** 5 yd
8. length of a rug in your living room	**a.** 5 in.	**b.** 5 ft	**c.** 5 mi
9. distance you can ride your bike	**a.** 2 in.	**b.** 2 yd	**c.** 2 mi
10. length of someone's foot	**a.** 8 in.	**b.** 8 yd	**c.** 8 mi
11. height of a finger puppet	**a.** 4 in.	**b.** 4 ft	**c.** 4 yd
12. length of your pencil	**a.** 5 in.	**b.** 5 ft	**c.** 5 yd
13. distance from your house to school	**a.** 2 in.	**b.** 20 ft	**c.** 2 mi
14. length of your calculator	**a.** 4 in.	**b.** 4 ft	**c.** 4 yd
15. height of a tree	**a.** 40 ft	**b.** 4 yd	**c.** 40 mi

RENAME CUSTOMARY UNITS OF LENGTH

Complete.

1.

Miles	1	2	3	4	5	6	7
Yards	1,760						

2. 60 in. = _____ ft

3. 9 ft = _____ yd

4. 4 ft = _____ in.

5. 4 yd = _____ ft

6. 8 ft = _____ in.

7. 24 in. = _____ ft

8. 1 mi = _____ yd

9. 21 ft = _____ yd

10. 5,280 yd = _____ mi

11. 3 ft = _____ in.

12. 6 yd = _____ ft

13. 36 in. = _____ yd

14. 2 yd = _____ in.

15. 3 yd = _____ in.

16. 5 yd = _____ ft

17. 10 yd = _____ ft

18. 7,040 yd = _____ mi

19. 6 ft = _____ in.

Write >, <, or =.

20. 1 ft ◯ 10 in.

21. 14 in. ◯ 3 yd

22. 36 in. ◯ 2 yd

23. 3 ft ◯ 35 in.

24. 10 ft ◯ 3 yd

25. 5 yd ◯ 15 ft

26. 3 ft ◯ 24 in.

27. 2 yd ◯ 3 ft

28. 1 ft ◯ 12 in.

29. 1 yd ◯ 3 ft

30. 4 ft ◯ 50 in.

31. 9 yd ◯ 26 ft

32. 1 yd ◯ 1 ft

33. 2 yd ◯ 6 ft

34. 4 ft ◯ 48 in.

35. 3 ft ◯ 13 in.

36. 1 mi ◯ 100 yd

37. 2 yd ◯ 73 in.

Solve.

38. Greg planted an orange seed 3 years ago when he was in first grade. The plant grew about 4 inches every year. About how tall in feet is the orange plant now?

39. Greg planted an evergreen tree 1 yard tall. He thinks that in 8 years the tree will be twice as tall. How many feet will that be? How many inches?

_____

_____

LENGTH IN METRIC UNITS

Estimate and then measure.

1. length of your thumb _____

2. length of your longest strand of hair _____

3. width of your math book _____

4. height of your desk _____

Ring the letter of the best estimate.

5. length of your shoe	**a.** 9 cm	**b.** 9 m	**c.** 9 km
6. distance you can jump	**a.** 1 cm	**b.** 1 dm	**c.** 1 m
7. distance from one town to another	**a.** 30 m	**b.** 30 km	**c.** 30 dm
8. length of a piece of chalk	**a.** 5 dm	**b.** 5 cm	**c.** 5 km
9. height of the door	**a.** 2 km	**b.** 2 m	**c.** 2 dm
10. length of a bicycle race	**a.** 5 cm	**b.** 5 m	**c.** 5 km

Complete.

11.

Kilometers	1	2	3	4	5	6
Meters	1,000					
Decimeters	10,000					

12. 8 cm = _____ mm 13. 2 m = _____ cm 14. 70 dm = _____ m

15. 5 m = _____ dm 16. 20 cm = _____ dm 17. 400 mm = _____ cm

18. 6 km = _____ m 19. 8,000 m = _____ km 20. 5 km = _____ m

21. 2 cm = _____ mm 22. 40 cm = _____ dm 23. 20 dm = _____ m

24. 30 dm = _____ m 25. 5,000 m = _____ km 26. 7,000 m = _____ km

McGraw-Hill School Division

Grade 4, Chapter 7, Lesson 3, pages 246–249

PERIMETER

Find the perimeter.

1.
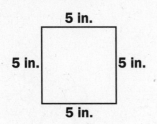

_____

2.
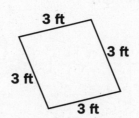

_____

3.
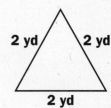

_____

4.
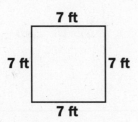

_____

5.
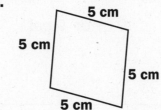

_____

6.
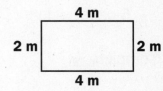

_____

Algebra Find the length of the missing side.

7.
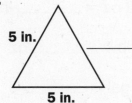

Perimeter = 15 in.

8.
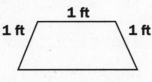

Perimeter = 5 ft

9.
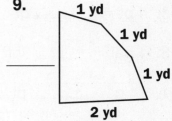

Perimeter = 7 yd

Solve.

10. Ernie's mother agreed to let him paint a triangle on his bedroom wall. He made two sides that were 6 feet long and one side that was 3 feet long. What is the perimeter of Ernie's triangle?

_____

11. Ernie also painted a make-believe window on another wall in his room. He made a rectangle that was 2 meters long and 1 meter high. What is the perimeter of the rectangle?

_____

CAPACITY AND WEIGHT IN CUSTOMARY UNITS

Ring the most reasonable estimate.

1.

5 oz or 5 lb

2.

9 qt or 9 gal

3.

7 oz or 7 lb

Complete.

4.

Pints	1	2	3	4	5	6
Cups	2					
Ounces	16					

5. 4 pt = _____ qt

6. 4 c = _____ qt

7. 32 oz = _____ lb

8. 1 gal = _____ qt

9. 9 gal = _____ qt

10. $\frac{1}{2}$ lb = _____ oz

11. 14 c = _____ pt

12. 12 pt = _____ qt

13. 2 gal = _____ c

14. 8 pt = _____ gal

15. 320 oz = _____ lb

16. 4 qt = _____ pt

17. 5 lb = _____ oz

18. 3 qt = _____ pt

19. 4 gal = _____ qt

Solve.

20. Emma buys 6 gallons of milk. If she buys the milk in 1-quart containers, how many containers does she buy?

_____

21. Emma buys a month's worth of food for her dog. Does she buy a 10-pound bag or a 10-ounce bag of dog food?

_____

Grade 4, Chapter 7, Lesson 5, pages 256–259

McGraw-Hill School Division

PROBLEM-SOLVING: USE LOGICAL REASONING

☑ Read
☑ Plan
☑ Solve
☑ Look Back

Solve using the logical-reasoning strategy.

1. Terry has been asked to make plaster of Paris for the class. She needs 6 quarts of water. She has a 5-quart jar and a 7-quart jar. How can she use them to measure 6 quarts?

_____

_____

_____

2. The class used all the plaster of Paris, and now Terry needs to make a larger amount. She has one 7-quart jar and one 5-quart jar. How can she use them to measure 9 quarts of water?

_____

_____

_____

3. Carlos makes 2 more plaster frogs than Tina. Tina makes 2 more than Maria, who makes twice as many as Jeff. If Jeff makes 6, how many do the others make?

_____

4. Keisha finishes her crafts project 15 minutes before David, who finishes 5 minutes after Mindy. Mindy finishes 20 minutes before Ben. Ben finishes at 10:30. When do the others finish?

_____

Solve using any method.

5. The class has been making papier-mâché fish all week. They use 5 pounds of papier-mâché. How many ounces of papier-mâché is that?

_____

6. Some of the students display their papier-mâché fish on a window ledge in the classroom. Each fish is 4 inches long, and the window ledge is 1 yard long. How many fish can fit on the ledge?

_____

CAPACITY AND MASS IN METRIC UNITS

Ring the most reasonable estimate.

1.

300 g or 30 g or 1 kg

2.

1 mL or 10 mL or 1 L

3.

1,800 kg or 8 kg or 180 kg

Complete.

4. 1 L = _____ mL

5. 1 kg = _____ g

6. 10 kg = _____ g

7. 30 kg = _____ g

8. 5,000 mL = _____ L

9. 20,000 mL = _____ L

10. 70 L = _____ mL

11. 60,000 g = _____ kg

12. 650 kg = _____ g

13. 4,000 g = _____ kg

14. 5 L = _____ mL

15. 9,000 mL = _____ L

16. 2 L = _____ mL

17. 3,000 g = _____ kg

18. 15 kg = _____ g

Solve.

19. Mattie uses 250,000 milligrams of fish food when she feeds the fish in the classroom. How many grams of fish food does she use?

_____

20. Mattie puts 5 liters of water in the fish bowl. Then she adds 600 milliliters of liquid fish vitamins. How much liquid in milliliters is in the fish bowl?

_____

PROBLEM SOLVING: CHECK FOR REASONABLENESS

Solve.

1. There is ice in your yard and snow is falling. The wind shakes the trees. Which temperature is reasonable, 75°F or 20°F?

2. You wear shorts and a T-shirt and sit in your yard in the shade of a tree. You want a cool breeze. Which temperature is reasonable, 5°C or 22°C?

3. You are boiling water to make hot chocolate. What is the temperature of the boiling water, 100°F or 212°F?

4. You are raking leaves in the fall wearing jeans and a sweatshirt. Which temperature is reasonable, 13°C or 25°C?

5. You want to buy a garden hose. You estimate that you will need a 2-foot-long hose. Is that reasonable? Why or why not?

6. You look at your flower garden. You think it must be 2 kilometers long. Is that reasonable? Why or why not? What might be more reasonable?

Solve using any method.

7. During hot weather, you water your flower garden with 10 gallons of water a day. How many gallons would you use in 3 weeks? Which operation did you use to solve this problem?

8. Your flower garden is 20 feet long and 15 feet wide. It also has a fence with a gate on each side. What is the perimeter of your flower garden? What information is not needed to find the perimeter?

MENTAL MATH: DIVISION PATTERNS

Divide mentally.

1. 20 ÷ 2 = _____

2. 60 ÷ 2 = _____

3. 80 ÷ 4 = _____

4. 90 ÷ 3 = _____

5. 150 ÷ 3 = _____

6. 210 ÷ 7 = _____

7. 250 ÷ 5 = _____

8. 180 ÷ 6 = _____

9. 2,400 ÷ 6 = _____

10. 630 ÷ 7 = _____

11. 1,600 ÷ 4 = _____

12. 640 ÷ 8 = _____

13. 4,500 ÷ 9 = _____

14. 320 ÷ 8 = _____

15. 3,200 ÷ 8 = _____

16. 1,800 ÷ 3 = _____

17. 2,000 ÷ 4 = _____

18. 4,200 ÷ 7 = _____

19. 5,400 ÷ 9 = _____

20. 720 ÷ 8 = _____

21. 8,100 ÷ 9 = _____

22. 4,900 ÷ 7 = _____

23. 4,800 ÷ 8 = _____

24. 3,600 ÷ 6 = _____

25. 4,000 ÷ 5 = _____

26. 1,800 ÷ 9 = _____

27. 5,600 ÷ 8 = _____

28. 6,300 ÷ 9 = _____

29. 1,400 ÷ 7 = _____

30. 2,800 ÷ 7 = _____

Algebra Find the missing number.

31. 45 ÷ _____ = 9

32. 450 ÷ _____ = 90

33. _____ ÷ 2 = 400

34. _____ ÷ 3 = 900

35. 320 ÷ _____ = 40

36. 4,800 ÷ _____ = 800

37. _____ ÷ 3 = 400

38. _____ ÷ 7 = 500

39. 2,700 ÷ _____ = 300

Solve mentally.

40. There will be 200 tap dancers in 4 groups performing in the Park School Hollywood Talent Show. All the groups will have an equal number of dancers. How many dancers will be in each group?

_____

41. Sixty actors will put on 6 funny skits at the Talent Show. All the skits will have an equal number of actors. How many actors will there be in each skit?

_____

MENTAL MATH: ESTIMATE QUOTIENTS

Estimate by using compatible numbers.
Explain your method.

1. 41 ÷ 2 _____ **2.** 70 ÷ 3 _____

3. 70 ÷ 4 _____ **4.** 362 ÷ 9 _____

5. 279 ÷ 3 _____ **6.** 237 ÷ 8 _____

7. 349 ÷ 7 _____ **8.** 430 ÷ 9 _____

9. 470 ÷ 6 _____ **10.** 563 ÷ 8 _____

11. 730 ÷ 9 _____ **12.** 642 ÷ 8 _____

13. 1,815 ÷ 6 _____ **14.** 3,255 ÷ 4 _____

15. 2,523 ÷ 5 _____ **16.** 5,511 ÷ 7 _____

17. 8,321 ÷ 9 _____ **18.** 5,420 ÷ 6 _____

19. 2,045 ÷ 3 _____ **20.** 1,209 ÷ 5 _____

21. 6,234 ÷ 7 _____ **22.** 2,978 ÷ 4 _____

23. 7,389 ÷ 9 _____ **24.** 5,005 ÷ 7 _____

Solve.

25. Your family travels a total of 94 miles to El Paso, Texas, every week for shopping. If you go 3 times a week, about how many miles is each round trip to El Paso?

26. Your parents once took a bike trip of 183 miles to Jasper, Wyoming. It took them 9 days. About how many miles did they travel each day?

_____

_____

DIVISION BY 1-DIGIT NUMBERS

Write a division sentence to represent the models.

1.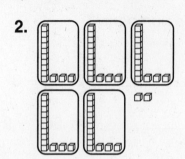

_____

2.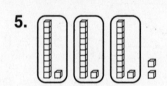

_____

3.

_____

4.

_____

5.

_____

6.

_____

Divide. You may use place-value models.

7. $19 \div 6 =$ _____

8. $35 \div 4 =$ _____

9. $29 \div 8 =$ _____

10. $32 \div 9 =$ _____

11. $40 \div 9 =$ _____

12. $60 \div 9 =$ _____

13. $49 \div 4 =$ _____

14. $64 \div 5 =$ _____

15. $79 \div 6 =$ _____

16. $82 \div 7 =$ _____

17. $98 \div 6 =$ _____

18. $99 \div 7 =$ _____

19. $53 \div 2 =$ _____

20. $97 \div 2 =$ _____

21. $89 \div 3 =$ _____

22. $59 \div 7 =$ _____

23. $28 \div 3 =$ _____

24. $38 \div 5 =$ _____

25. $17 \div 2 =$ _____

26. $41 \div 9 =$ _____

27. $20 \div 6 =$ _____

28. $29 \div 5 =$ _____

29. $62 \div 7 =$ _____

30. $53 \div 6 =$ _____

McGraw-Hill School Division

DIVISION BY 1-DIGIT NUMBERS

Divide. Remember to estimate.

1. 2)80   **2.** 3)210   **3.** 5)450   **4.** 9)810

5. 3)47   **6.** 2)31   **7.** 4)53   **8.** 2)79

9. 2)93   **10.** 7)96   **11.** 6)69   **12.** 3)91

13. 6)473   **14.** 5)364   **15.** 4)290   **16.** 6)299

17. 4)$375   **18.** 7)$646   **19.** 9)$872   **20.** 4)$896

21. 5)665   **22.** 8)453   **23.** 3)265   **24.** 2)625

Algebra Ring the letter of the missing number.

25. $85 \div \square = 12 \text{ R } 1$ **a.** 6   **b.** 7   **c.** 8   **d.** 9

26. $\square \div 9 = 50$ **a.** 45   **b.** 450   **c.** 400   **d.** 540

27. $46 \div \square = 15 \text{ R1}$ **a.** 2   **b.** 5   **c.** 6   **d.** 3

28. $\square \div 8 = 7 \text{ R5}$ **a.** 65   **b.** 56   **c.** 51   **d.** 61

29. $67 \div \square = 6 \text{ R1}$ **a.** 9   **b.** 10   **c.** 11   **d.** 12

Solve.

30. Ann has a roll of 159 stickers. She pastes an equal number in 7 different notebooks. How many does Ann put in each notebook? How many are left over?

31. Ann's story notebook has 215 pages. If she fills it with 4-page stories, how many stories will she have? How many pages will be left over?

_____   _____

ZEROS IN THE QUOTIENT

Divide.

1. 4)418

2. 6)616

3. 2)405

4. 2)603

5. 5)526

6. 2)817

7. 6)241

8. 7)762

9. 3)319

10. 4)835

11. 5)$550

12. 3)$902

13. 2)340

14. 4)423

15. 2)617

16. 7)768

17. 8)853

18. 7)710

19. 9)985

20. 6)584

21. 3)925

22. 8)562

23. 4)814

24. 5)654

How many:

25. $5 are in $200? _____

26. $5 are in $450? _____

27. $6 are in $618? _____

28. $7 are in $735? _____

29. $3 are in $306? _____

30. $2 are in $406? _____

31. $2 are in $960? _____

32. $3 are in $609? _____

Solve.

33. Francis earns $535 in 5 months by selling maps and guidebooks to tourists. If divided evenly, how much is that a month?

34. A family of 4 spends $436 during their vacation. How much money does one person spend if they all spend the same amount?

_____

_____

DIVIDE GREATER NUMBERS

Divide.

1. 7)892 **2.** 9)733 **3.** 5)615 **4.** 8)868

5. 4)279 **6.** 7)3,546 **7.** 5)1,205 **8.** 7)3,026

9. 6)6,094 **10.** 3)$3,019 **11.** 4)8,704

12. 3)28,602 **13.** 8)40,969 **14.** 9)70,235

Find only those quotients that are greater than 600.

15. 4)2,432 **16.** 9)6,246 **17.** 9)5,290 **18.** 2)1,628

19. 6)2,562 **20.** 5)3,567 **21.** 3)2,587 **22.** 4)2,527

23. 8)6,016 **24.** 7)4,196 **25.** 8)4,992 **26.** 6)2,927

27. 7)5,613 **28.** 9)5,321 **29.** 6)4,002 **30.** 8)5,760

31. 6)4,535 **32.** 5)3,013 **33.** 4)2,244 **34.** 9)5,596

Solve.

35. Your family collects 1,071 photographs from 7 summers together. If you took the same number of photographs each year, how many photographs are there for each summer?

36. During 3 summers, your family travels 2,052 miles going to and from the same camping area. How many miles did you travel in one summer? How many miles is it one way?

_____ _____

McGraw-Hill School Division

PROBLEM-SOLVING STRATEGY: GUESS, TEST, AND REVISE

☑ Read
☑ Plan
☑ Solve
☑ Look Back

Solve using the guess, test, and revise strategy.

1. Your family bikes and camps in Vermont for 5 days. You cover 22 miles by going either 4 or 5 miles a day. On how many days do you travel 4 miles? 5 miles?

2. Your brother has the task of dividing 20 snacks between you and 3 friends. He wants you to have twice as many as any of the others. How many snacks do you get? How many do the others get?

3. While biking, you drink 19 ounces of a juice and water mixture that you prepared. It contains 3 more ounces of water than juice. How many ounces of water do you drink?

4. You spent $3 or $4 a day on snacks in small towns while on the bike trip. If you spent $17 during the 5 days, on how many days did you spend $3? $4?

Solve using any method.

5. A forest ranger tells you that about 1,300 cars used a nearby highway over a recent 4-day holiday weekend. Estimate the number of cars per day.

6. You stop at a bookstore in a small town to buy a Bike Traveler's Manual. It has 1,035 pages. You plan to read 5 pages a night. How many nights will it take?

7. By saving all year, your family has $1,002 to spend on this vacation trip. By the third night, you have spent $499. How much is left to spend? How much is that for each of 2 days?

8. To plan for next year's vacation, your parents have decided to save $140 each month for 9 months. Your brother will save $3.75 and you will save $0.35 each month. How much is that in all?

McGraw-Hill School Division

AVERAGE

Find the average.

1. Number of trips you made to a neighboring state in the last four years: 3, 8, 6, 3

   _____

2. Number of books you have read about your own state each year: 3, 7, 5

   _____

3. Number of rolls of film used in a week on a summer vacation: 4, 2, 4, 1, 4

   _____

4. Number of gallons of gas used per day: 11, 10, 5, 15, 11, 8

   _____

5. Number of friends you talked to on the phone about a vacation trip: 6, 3, 1, 2

   _____

6. Number of times your family stopped each day on your trip: 6, 3, 3, 4, 6, 2

   _____

7. Amount of money your family spent on hotels and motels: $65, $120, $100, $105, $70, $122

   _____

8. Number of pictures you took each day of your vacation: 0, 24, 31, 10, 15, 11, 9, 2, 6

   _____

9. Number of miles traveled each day: 325, 475, 650, 500, 275, 379

   _____

10. Number of seashells collected by each family member: 29, 17, 36, 8, 15

    _____

Solve. You may use snap cubes.

11. Your class collected pictures and other items about your state. The number of things brought in to class each day was: 35, 28, 5, 10, 2. What was the average number of items brought in each day?

    _____

12. Your school has special Celebrate-Our-State days. For the last 4 years, the school spent $240, $362, $409, and $205 on the festival. What was the average amount of money spent a year?

    _____

MENTAL MATH: DIVIDE BY MULTIPLES OF TEN

Divide mentally.

1. 160 ÷ 4 = _____   **2.** 120 ÷ 40 = _____   **3.** 1,200 ÷ 40 = _____

4. 90 ÷ 30 = _____   **5.** 60 ÷ 10 = _____   **6.** 600 ÷ 30 = _____

7. 350 ÷ 70 = _____   **8.** 560 ÷ 70 = _____   **9.** 3,500 ÷ 70 = _____

10. 720 ÷ 80 = _____   **11.** 360 ÷ 60 = _____   **12.** 7,200 ÷ 80 = _____

13. 270 ÷ 90 = _____   **14.** 810 ÷ 90 = _____   **15.** 300 ÷ 50 = _____

16. $360 ÷ 90 = _____   **17.** $200 ÷ 50 = _____   **18.** 540 ÷ 90 = _____

19. 1,800 ÷ 20 = _____ **20.** 3,000 ÷ 50 = _____ **21.** 30,000 ÷ 50 = _____

22. $4,000 ÷ 50 = _____ **23.** 54,000 ÷ 60 = _____ **24.** $2,800 ÷ 70 = _____

25. 49,000 ÷ 70 = _____ **26.** $2,000 ÷ 40 = _____ **27.** $20,000 ÷ 50 = _____

28. 6,300 ÷ 70 = _____ **29.** 14,000 ÷ 70 = _____ **30.** 48,000 ÷ 60 = _____

Algebra Find the missing number.

31. 80 ÷ _____ = 2   **32.** 450 ÷ _____ = 5   **33.** 320 ÷ 80 = _____

34. _____ ÷ 60 = 4   **35.** _____ ÷ 70 = 7   **36.** 400 ÷ _____ = 8

37. 180 ÷ _____ = 3   **38.** _____ ÷ 20 = 30   **39.** _____ ÷ 40 = 90

Solve.

40. The teachers have 270 animal picture cards to be divided among 30 fourth graders. How many does each student get?

41. There are 3,200 "Save the Rain Forests" pins given to 80 different school classes. How many pins does each class get?

_____   _____

DIVIDE BY TENS

Complete the division sentence.

1.

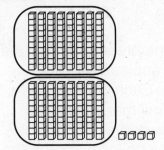

164 ÷ 80 = _____

2.

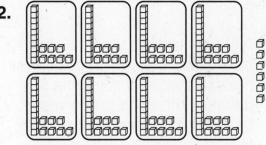

142 ÷ 17 = _____

3.

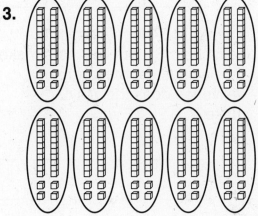

240 ÷ 10 = _____

4.

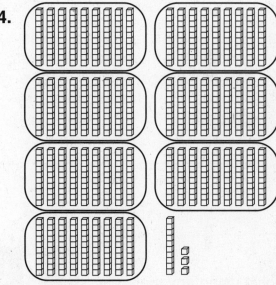

643 ÷ 90 = _____

Divide using any method.

5. 13)‾84   **6.** 15)‾32   **7.** 18)‾93   **8.** 16)‾79

9. 62 ÷ 17 = _____   **10.** 77 ÷ 25 = _____   **11.** 85 ÷ 14 = _____

12. 99 ÷ 23 = _____   **13.** 152 ÷ 13 = _____   **14.** 204 ÷ 17 = _____

15. $204 ÷ 18 = _____   **16.** $210 ÷ 29 = _____   **17.** 372 ÷ 23 = _____

Name: _____

PROBLEM SOLVING: INTERPRET THE QUOTIENT AND REMAINDER

✔ Read
✔ Plan
✔ Solve
✔ Look Back

Solve.

1. A charity organization delivers boxes of apples. Each box can hold 35 apples. If someone donates 180 apples, how many boxes can be completely filled? How many apples will be left over?

_____

2. People volunteer to deliver the boxes of apples to different locations. Each car can carry 4 boxes. How many cars are needed to deliver 122 boxes? How many boxes will be in the last car?

_____

3. Each location receives 8 boxes of apples. If there are 219 boxes, how many locations will receive 8 boxes? How many boxes are left over?

_____

4. There are 34 locations for the deliveries. Six out of 7 cars make 5 deliveries each. How many deliveries does the 7th car make?

_____

Solve using any method.

5. A school bus uses 1 gallon of gasoline to travel 9 miles. How many gallons does it use to travel 180 miles?

_____

6. A school bus uses 1 tank of gasoline to travel 200 miles. About how many tanks does it use to travel 760 miles?

_____

7. A school bus travels 150 miles in 5 days. How many miles does it travel in 1 day if it travels the same number of miles each day?

_____

8. If a school bus travels 600 miles each month, how many miles does it travel in 6 months?

_____

Grade 4, Chapter 8, Lesson 11, pages 308–311

3-DIMENSIONAL FIGURES

Name the 3-dimensional figure the object looks like.

1.

_____

2.

_____

3.

_____

4.

_____

5.

_____

6.

_____

7.

_____

8.

_____

9.

_____

Describe the figure. Tell how many edges, vertices, and faces it has.

10.

_____

_____

11.

_____

_____

12.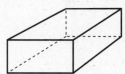

_____

_____

13.

_____

_____

14.

_____

_____

15.

_____

_____

2-DIMENSIONAL FIGURES AND POLYGONS

Tell if the figure is open or closed.

1.

_____

2.

_____

3.

_____

4.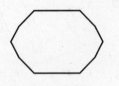

_____

5.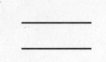

_____

6.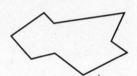

_____

Name the polygon.

7.

_____

8.

_____

9.

_____

10.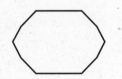

_____

11.

_____

12.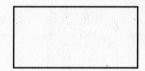

_____

13.

_____

14.

_____

15.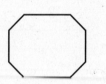

_____

Solve.

16. A stop sign is shaped

like a(n) _____ .

17. A yield sign is shaped

like a(n) _____ .

McGraw-Hill School Division

LINE SEGMENTS, LINES, AND RAYS

Describe the figure.

1.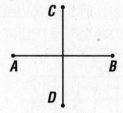

2.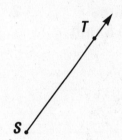

3.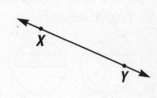

_____

4.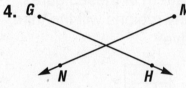

5.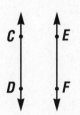

6.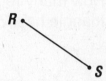

_____

7.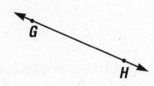

8.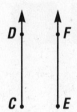

9.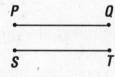

_____

Solve.

10. Name all the line segments in the picture.

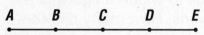

_____

11. Draw six lines with one point in common.

McGraw-Hill School Division

PROBLEM-SOLVING STRATEGY: MAKE AN ORGANIZED LIST

✔ **Read**
✔ **Plan**
✔ **Solve**
✔ **Look Back**

Solve using the make-an-organized-list strategy.

1. Find a pattern in these figures. How many regions will the fourth circle have?

2. Find a pattern in this folded sheet of paper. How many regions will the fourth sheet have?

3. Find a pattern in these figures. How many regions will the fourth triangle have?

4. Find a pattern in these figures. How many regions will the third figure have?

Solve using any method.

5. Your class buys 6 boxes of sidewalk chalk. There are 20 pieces in each box. If there are 29 students in your class, about how many pieces of chalk will each student get?

6. There are 80 boxes of chalk for the fourth grade. There are 10 boxes of chalk for each class. If each class has about 20 students, how many students are there?

7. Your class has $20 and you want to buy more sidewalk chalk. If each box costs $3.25, how many boxes can you buy?

8. Kim uses red, yellow, and green chalk to shade a figure of 3 regions. How many different ways could she shade the figure?

McGraw-Hill School Division

ANGLES

Write *acute, obtuse,* or *right* for the angle.

1.

_____

2.

_____

3.

_____

4.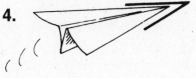

_____

5.

_____

6.

_____

Ring the letter that best describes the polygon.

7.

  a. 2 acute angles, 2 right angles, 1 pair of parallel lines

  b. 4 acute angles, 2 pairs of parallel lines

  c. 4 right angles, 2 pairs of parallel lines

8.

  a. 2 right angles, 1 acute angle, 3 intersecting lines

  b. 3 acute angles, 3 intersecting lines

  c. 3 acute angles, 3 perpendicular lines

9.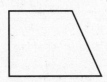

  a. 1 right angle, 2 acute angles, 1 obtuse angle, 2 pairs of parallel lines

  b. 2 right angles, 2 acute angles, 1 pair of parallel lines

  c. 2 right angles, 1 acute angle, 1 obtuse angle, 1 pair of parallel lines

10.

  a. 1 right angle, 2 acute angles, 1 pair of perpendicular lines

  b. 3 right angles, 3 intersecting lines

  c. 1 right angle, 1 acute angle, 1 obtuse angle

Name: _____

CONGRUENCY AND SIMILARITY

Is each figure *congruent* or *similar* to the original figure?

1.   **a.** 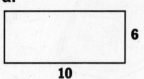   **b.** 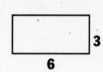   **c.**

_____

2.   **a.**   **b.**   **c.**

_____

3.   **a.** 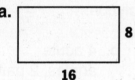   **b.**   **c.**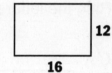

_____

4.   **a.**   **b.**   **c.**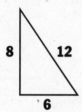

_____

Draw the figure on dot paper. Then draw a congruent and a similar figure.

5.    **6.**   **7.**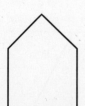

SYMMETRY

Is the dashed line a line of symmetry?

1.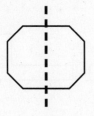

_____

2.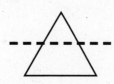

_____

3.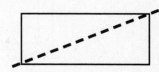

_____

4.

_____

5.

_____

6.

_____

Complete the figure to make it symmetrical.
Draw its line of symmetry.

7.

8.

9.

Solve.

10. Tell what polygon a TV remote
control resembles and how it is
symmetrical.

_____

_____

_____

_____

11. Tell what polygon a slice of pizza
resembles and how it is
symmetrical.

_____

_____

_____

_____

SLIDES, FLIPS, AND TURNS

Write *flip*, *slide*, or *turn* to tell how the figure was moved.

1.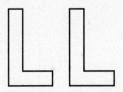

_____

2.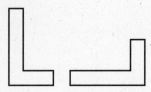

_____

3.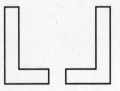

_____

4.

_____

5.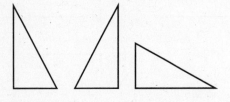

_____

6.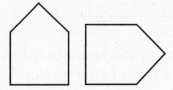

_____

Move the figure in the way indicated.

7. slide

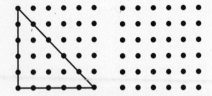

8. flip

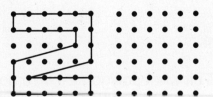

9. turn, then slide

10. flip, then turn

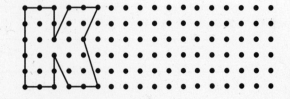

AREA

Find the area of the rectangles.

1.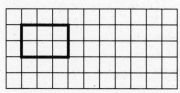

_____

2.

_____

3.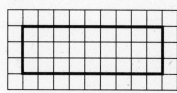

_____

4.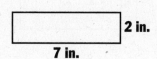

2 in.

7 in.

_____

5.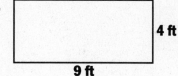

4 ft

9 ft

_____

6.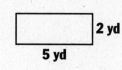

2 yd

5 yd

_____

7.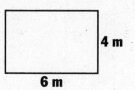

4 m

6 m

_____

8.

3 cm

3 cm

_____

9.

5 in.

7 in.

_____

Use graph paper to draw rectangles with the following areas.
How many rectangles are possible for each?

10. 15 square units

_____
_____

11. 12 square units

_____
_____

12. 16 square units

_____
_____

13. 27 square units

_____
_____

14. 30 square units

_____
_____

15. 40 square units

_____
_____

Name: _____

VOLUME

Find the volume for each rectangular prism.

1.

_____

2.

_____

3.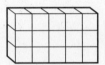

_____

4.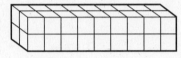

_____

5.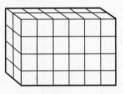

_____

6.

_____

7.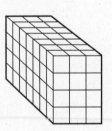

_____

8.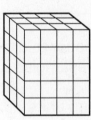

_____

9. length = 4 in.
width = 3 in.
height = 9 in.

_____

10. length = 5 m
width = 8 m
height = 7 m

_____

11. length = 8 cm
width = 2 cm
height = 9 cm

_____

12. length = 10 ft
width = 12 ft
height = 5 ft

_____

PROBLEM SOLVING: USE DIAGRAMS

✔ Read
✔ Plan
✔ Solve
✔ Look Back

Draw each figure in the Venn diagram.

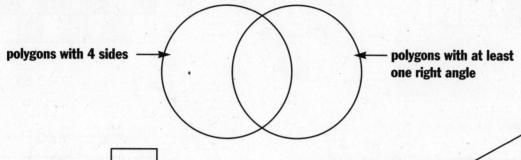

polygons with 4 sides → ← polygons with at least one right angle

1. square

2. right triangle

3. trapezoid

4. quadrilateral

5. pentagon

6. rectangle

Solve using any method.

7. Max's little brother, Rudy, has 144 blocks. He fits 6 rows of 8 blocks in the bottom of a box. How many more layers can he make?

_____

_____

_____

8. Max stacks 6 blocks. One orange is on top, and another orange is below a blue that is below a green. One red is above another blue and below an orange. What is the order of the blocks starting from the bottom?

_____

_____

_____

PART OF A WHOLE

Write the fraction for the part that is shaded.

1.

_____

2.

_____

3.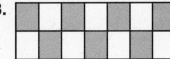

_____

4.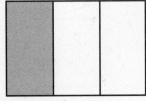

_____

5.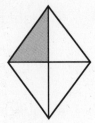

_____

6.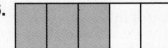

_____

7.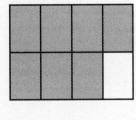

_____

8.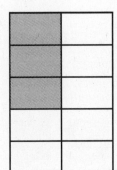

_____

9.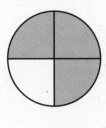

_____

Measure to the nearest fraction of an inch shown.

10. _____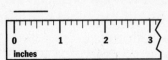

the nearest $\frac{1}{4}$ in.

_____

11. _____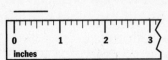

the nearest $\frac{1}{2}$ in.

_____

12. _____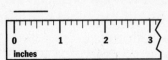

the nearest $\frac{1}{8}$ in.

_____

McGraw-Hill School Division

PART OF A GROUP

Choose the fraction that tells which part has no design.

1. ○○○◍◍◍◍◍●●   **2.** △△△△△△△△   **3.** ☺☺☺○○☹☹

a. $\frac{4}{10}$ **a.** $\frac{2}{5}$ **a.** $\frac{2}{7}$

b. $\frac{3}{10}$ **b.** $\frac{1}{8}$ **b.** $\frac{3}{7}$

c. $\frac{3}{7}$ **c.** $\frac{5}{8}$ **c.** $\frac{4}{7}$

Draw a picture. Then write the fraction.

4. Three out of eight students are laughing.

5. Two out of five students are winking.

6. Four out of seven students are sitting.

7. Five out of six students are standing.

Solve.

8. Seven students out of 19 want to play Red Rover. What part of the group wants to play Red Rover?

9. Nine students out of 23 vote to play kickball. What part of the whole group votes for kickball?

FIND A FRACTION OF A NUMBER

Use the picture to help you find the missing number or fraction.

1. ○○○   ⬭   **2.** ○○○   ⬭   **3.** ⬭ ⬭ ⬭

$\frac{1}{3}$ of 9 = _____ $\frac{3}{4}$ of 12 = _____ $\frac{6}{7}$ of 14 = _____

4.   **5.**   **6.**

$\frac{2}{5}$ of 20 = _____ $\frac{1}{3}$ of 18 = _____ $\frac{5}{7}$ of 21 = _____

Find the answer. Use any method.

7. $\frac{2}{3}$ of 9 = _____   **8.** $\frac{3}{4}$ of 16 = _____   **9.** $\frac{2}{3}$ of 12 = _____

10. $\frac{5}{8}$ of 16 = _____   **11.** $\frac{2}{3}$ of 18 = _____   **12.** $\frac{1}{5}$ of 15 = _____

13. _____ of 20 = 18   **14.** _____ of 21 = 12   **15.** _____ of 27 = 9

Solve. You may use counters.

16. Keisha wins 30 games of Flash Card Race. She played $\frac{2}{5}$ of those games with fifth graders. How many games is that?

_____

17. Of the 21 fourth graders, $\frac{1}{3}$ like to play football. How many students is that?

_____

EQUIVALENT FRACTIONS

Complete and name the equivalent fraction. You may use fractions strips.

1.

| $\frac{1}{8}$ | $\frac{1}{8}$ | $\frac{1}{8}$ | $\frac{1}{8}$ |

| $\frac{1}{2}$ |

$\frac{4}{8} = \frac{\square}{2}$

2.

| $\frac{1}{6}$ |

| $\frac{1}{12}$ | $\frac{1}{12}$ |

$\frac{1}{6} = \frac{\square}{12}$

3.

| $\frac{1}{5}$ |

| $\frac{1}{10}$ | $\frac{1}{10}$ |

$\frac{1}{5} = \frac{\square}{10}$

4.

| $\frac{1}{6}$ | $\frac{1}{6}$ | $\frac{1}{6}$ | $\frac{1}{6}$ | $\frac{1}{6}$ |

| $\frac{1}{12}$ | $\frac{1}{12}$ | $\frac{1}{12}$ | $\frac{1}{12}$ | $\frac{1}{12}$ | $\frac{1}{12}$ | $\frac{1}{12}$ | $\frac{1}{12}$ | $\frac{1}{12}$ | $\frac{1}{12}$ |

$\frac{5}{6} = \frac{10}{\square}$

5.

| $\frac{1}{10}$ | $\frac{1}{10}$ | $\frac{1}{10}$ | $\frac{1}{10}$ | $\frac{1}{10}$ |

| $\frac{1}{2}$ |

$\frac{5}{10} = \frac{\square}{2}$

6.

| $\frac{1}{12}$ | $\frac{1}{12}$ | $\frac{1}{12}$ | $\frac{1}{12}$ |

| $\frac{1}{3}$ |

$\frac{4}{12} = \frac{1}{\square}$

7. $\frac{3}{12} = \frac{\square}{4}$

8. $\frac{2}{3} = \frac{8}{\square}$

9. $\frac{3}{4} = \frac{\square}{8}$

Complete.

10. $\frac{1 \times \square}{4 \times \square} = \frac{2}{8}$

11. $\frac{2 \times \square}{3 \times \square} = \frac{6}{9}$

12. $\frac{4 \times \square}{5 \times \square} = \frac{8}{10}$

13. $\frac{9}{10} = \frac{18}{\square}$

14. $\frac{5}{20} = \frac{1}{\square}$

15. $\frac{5}{8} = \frac{\square}{24}$

Solve.

16. Vicky had $\frac{3}{4}$ of a pie. She wants to serve it to 6 people. How many eighths of the pie does she serve?

_____

17. Bill eats 2 out of 8 carrots. Name an equivalent fraction.

_____

SIMPLIFY FRACTIONS

Complete to show the simplest form.

1.

$\frac{2}{4} = \frac{\square}{\square}$

2.

$\frac{3}{6} = \frac{\square}{\square}$

3.

$\frac{2}{6} = \frac{\square}{\square}$

4.

$\frac{6}{10} = \frac{\square}{\square}$

5.

$\frac{6}{8} = \frac{\square}{\square}$

6.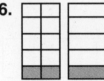

$\frac{2}{10} = \frac{\square}{\square}$

Write the fraction in simplest form.

7. $\frac{4}{8}$ _____

8. $\frac{4}{10}$ _____

9. $\frac{3}{12}$ _____

10. $\frac{5}{10}$ _____

11. $\frac{8}{12}$ _____

12. $\frac{4}{24}$ _____

13. $\frac{10}{45}$ _____

14. $\frac{14}{49}$ _____

15. $\frac{32}{36}$ _____

16. $\frac{4}{16}$ _____

17. $\frac{3}{27}$ _____

18. $\frac{6}{15}$ _____

19. $\frac{3}{18}$ _____

20. $\frac{4}{12}$ _____

21. $\frac{8}{24}$ _____

22. $\frac{10}{12}$ _____

Solve.

23. Ann practices scooping up more than one jack at a time from 10. First, she bounces the ball and picks up 2 jacks. What fraction of 10 is that? Write the fraction in simplest form.

_____

24. Maska and Dan played 6 games of table tennis. Maska won 2 of the games and Dan won 4. What fraction of the games did each win? Write the fractions in simplest form.

_____

Grade 4, Chapter 10, Lesson 5, pages 380–381

McGraw-Hill School Division

COMPARE FRACTIONS

Write >, <, or =. Use mental math when you can.

1. $\frac{1}{2}$ ◯ $\frac{5}{10}$

2. $\frac{3}{4}$ ◯ $\frac{1}{2}$

3. $\frac{2}{3}$ ◯ $\frac{3}{9}$

4. $\frac{8}{16}$ ◯ $\frac{3}{4}$

5. $\frac{15}{30}$ ◯ $\frac{10}{20}$

6. $\frac{1}{4}$ ◯ $\frac{2}{12}$

7. $\frac{2}{4}$ ◯ $\frac{6}{8}$

8. $\frac{2}{3}$ ◯ $\frac{8}{12}$

9. $\frac{3}{5}$ ◯ $\frac{14}{20}$

10. $\frac{5}{8}$ ◯ $\frac{1}{4}$

11. $\frac{2}{3}$ ◯ $\frac{1}{6}$

12. $\frac{3}{7}$ ◯ $\frac{8}{21}$

13. $\frac{3}{10}$ ◯ $\frac{2}{5}$

14. $\frac{5}{6}$ ◯ $\frac{10}{12}$

15. $\frac{6}{20}$ ◯ $\frac{3}{10}$

16. $\frac{3}{4}$ ◯ $\frac{9}{12}$

17. $\frac{2}{20}$ ◯ $\frac{1}{5}$

18. $\frac{8}{14}$ ◯ $\frac{1}{2}$

Write in order from greatest to least.

19. $\frac{5}{8}, \frac{1}{4}, \frac{1}{2}$ _____

20. $\frac{1}{2}, \frac{1}{8}, \frac{5}{8}$ _____

21. $\frac{3}{8}, \frac{1}{8}, \frac{1}{2}$ _____

22. $\frac{1}{2}, \frac{3}{4}, \frac{1}{8}$ _____

23. $\frac{3}{7}, \frac{1}{7}, \frac{5}{7}$ _____

24. $\frac{1}{9}, \frac{1}{3}, \frac{2}{3}$ _____

25. $\frac{1}{2}, \frac{3}{4}, \frac{1}{4}$ _____

26. $\frac{1}{9}, \frac{7}{9}, \frac{2}{9}$ _____

27. $\frac{1}{4}, \frac{1}{8}, \frac{3}{8}$ _____

28. $\frac{2}{3}, \frac{1}{6}, \frac{1}{3}$ _____

Solve.

29. Nate ate $\frac{3}{8}$ of the pizza and Jane ate $\frac{1}{4}$ of the pizza. Who ate more pizza?

_____

30. Paul had $\frac{1}{2}$ of a bowl of soup. Tim had $\frac{2}{3}$ of a bowl, and Kelly had $\frac{3}{4}$ of a bowl. Order the amount from least to greatest.

_____

MIXED NUMBERS

Describe the shaded part as a fraction and as a whole or a mixed number.

1.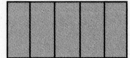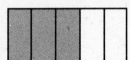

_____

2.

_____

3.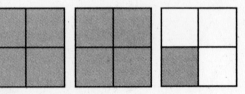

_____

4.

_____

Rename as a whole number or as a mixed number in simplest form.

5. $\frac{3}{3}$ _____

6. $\frac{5}{5}$ _____

7. $\frac{6}{5}$ _____

8. $\frac{9}{7}$ _____

9. $\frac{7}{7}$ _____

10. $\frac{6}{3}$ _____

11. $\frac{9}{3}$ _____

12. $\frac{10}{3}$ _____

13. $\frac{24}{6}$ _____

14. $\frac{25}{6}$ _____

15. $\frac{13}{4}$ _____

16. $\frac{31}{5}$ _____

17. $\frac{21}{14}$ _____

18. $\frac{24}{18}$ _____

19. $\frac{36}{18}$ _____

20. $\frac{27}{3}$ _____

21. $\frac{30}{7}$ _____

22. $\frac{48}{9}$ _____

23. $\frac{50}{8}$ _____

24. $\frac{75}{9}$ _____

Solve.

25. Wanda used $\frac{5}{3}$ cups of sugar in a cake recipe she was making. Write this as a whole or a mixed number.

_____

26. Ben used $\frac{16}{4}$ cups of milk in a dessert he was making. Write this as a whole or a mixed number.

_____

PROBABILITY

For exercises 1–13, write the words *more likely, less likely, equally likely, certain,* or *impossible* to describe the probability.

Use the picture to the right for exercises 1–5 .

1. choosing a circle

   _____

2. choosing a triangle

   _____

3. choosing a square or a star

   _____

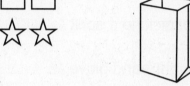

4. choosing a heart

   _____

5. choosing a circle if you had only

   circles in the bag _____

Use the spinner to the right for exercises 6–11.

6. spinning 5 _____
7. spinning 5 or not spinning 5

   _____

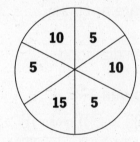

8. spinning 20 in one spin

   _____

9. spinning 10 in one spin

   _____

10. spinning 15 in one spin

    _____

11. not spinning 15

    _____

Solve.

12. Howard is given 8 apples and 2 oranges in a bag. Is it more likely, less likely, or equally likely that Howard will pick an orange?

    _____

13. In one bag, there are 11 good apples and 1 rotten apple. How likely is it that Rosa will pick the rotten apple?

    _____

FRACTIONS AND PROBABILITY

Find the probability of picking each item. Use the pictures below.

1. red crayon _____

2. green crayon _____

3. blue crayon _____

4. brown crayon _____

5. *not* an orange crayon _____

6. one mitten _____

7. *not* picking a sock _____

8. one sneaker _____

9. a right-hand glove _____

10. *not* picking a sneaker _____

11. a small shape _____

12. a large square _____

13. a star _____

14. a small star _____

15. a square or circle _____

16. a triangle _____

17. a small diamond _____

18. *not* a circle _____

Exercises 1–5	**Exercises 6–10**	**Exercises 11–18**

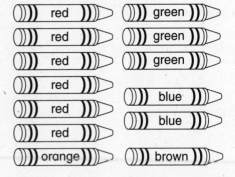  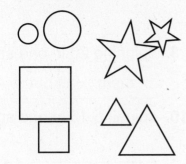

Solve.

19. Lisa has a coin in one hand. Both hands are behind her back. What is the probability of Jason guessing which hand the coin is in?

_____

20. Lisa turns over 6 cups. She hides the coin under one of them. What is the probability of Jason guessing which cup the coin is under?

_____

PROBLEM-SOLVING STRATEGY: CONDUCT AN EXPERIMENT

✔	Read
✔	Plan
✔	Solve
✔	Look Back

Solve using the conduct-an-experiment strategy.

1. Which combinations of heads and tails will come up most often if you toss 2 coins 60 times? Will it be heads/heads, tails/tails, or heads/tails?

_____

2. What if you place 1 red, 1 blue, and 2 green crayons in a bag? Then you have a friend take out one crayon, record the color, and put it back. What do you predict will happen if this is done several times? Check your prediction.

_____

3. You have 2 spinners. Each is numbered 4, 5, 6, 7, 10, 11, 14. If you spin both spinners 20 times and find the sum of each spin, which sums are likely to appear most often?

_____

4. If you toss 2 number cubes 20 times, how many times might you get multiples of 2 in each sum? How about 3? Make a prediction and check it.

_____

Solve using any method.

5. Leroy wants to fix up 35 of his toy cars to give away. He paints 21 of them. Half of the remaining cars need new wheels. How many cars need new wheels?

_____

6. Leroy promises a day care center that he will help them collect 60 repaired toys. So far he has collected 2 toys each from 27 students. How far along is Leroy in keeping his promise?

_____

7. Leroy's neighbor gives him 9 boxes of 8 magic markers. He has enough to give 3 markers to each child at the day care center. How many children are there?

_____

8. A business gives Leroy $1,000 to help with his day care center work. Leroy gives $500 to the day care center and spends $399 on books for the center. How much does he have left? _____

PREDICT AND EXPERIMENT

Use the spinner for problems 1–6. Write *true* or *false*. Explain your reasoning.

The probability of

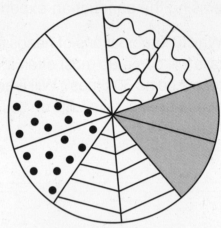

1. landing on a shaded section is $\frac{2}{10}$.

_____

2. not landing on a shaded section is $\frac{2}{10}$.

_____

3. not landing on white is $\frac{1}{5}$.

_____

4. landing on any of 3 designs is $\frac{3}{5}$.

_____

5. landing on a red section is 0.

_____

6. landing on dots or stripes is $\frac{3}{5}$.

_____

Use a number cube for problems 7–10. Explain your reasoning.

7. Predict the number of times a 4 will come up if you toss the number cube 30 times.

_____

_____

8. What if you double the number of cube tosses from 30 to 60? How often might 4 come up?

_____

_____

9. Is it reasonable to predict that you will toss a 6 on the number cube 2 out of 12 times?

_____

_____

10. Can you predict exactly how many times 4 will come up when you toss a number cube? Why?

_____

_____

PROBLEM SOLVING: SOLVE MULTISTEP PROBLEMS

✔	Read
✔	Plan
✔	Solve
✔	Look Back

Solve.

1. The fourth grade has a bake sale. They sell chocolate chip cookies for $2 a bag. If the ingredients cost $22 and the students sell 40 bags, how much do they make on chocolate chip cookies?

_____

2. The fourth grade sells 30 bags of brownies and 20 bags of oatmeal cookies. There are 3 brownies in a bag and 4 oatmeal cookies in a bag. How many brownies and oatmeal cookies are sold in all?

_____

3. The students bought 4 cases of 30 cartons of milk. If they sold 80 cartons, how many cases are left?

_____

4. Ten students brought 1 bottle of soda, and 3 students brought 2 bottles of soda. Aki brought the rest. If there were 19 bottles of soda in all, how many did Aki bring?

_____

Solve using any method.

5. Six students out of 18 in a class sing in the chorus after school. What fraction of the class sings in the chorus?

_____

6. One sixth of the students play in a baseball league after school. If there are 24 students in the class, how many play baseball?

_____

7. Tino and Bernie ride their bicycles for 5 miles every day after school. About how many miles do they ride in one month?

_____

8. Mary plays basketball for 2 hours after school. What fraction of one whole day does she spend playing basketball?

_____

ADD FRACTIONS

Add. Write a number sentence for each model.

1. $\boxed{\frac{1}{4}}$ $\boxed{\frac{1}{4}\,\frac{1}{4}}$

2. $\boxed{\frac{1}{5}\,\frac{1}{5}}$ $\boxed{\frac{1}{5}}$

3. $\boxed{\frac{1}{8}\,\frac{1}{8}\,\frac{1}{8}}$

$\boxed{\frac{1}{8}\,\frac{1}{8}\,\frac{1}{8}\,\frac{1}{8}\,\frac{1}{8}}$

_____

4. $\boxed{\frac{1}{6}\,\frac{1}{6}}$ $\boxed{\frac{1}{6}\,\frac{1}{6}}$

5. $\boxed{\frac{1}{10}\,\frac{1}{10}\,\frac{1}{10}\,\frac{1}{10}\,\frac{1}{10}\,\frac{1}{10}\,\frac{1}{10}}$

$\boxed{\frac{1}{10}\,\frac{1}{10}\,\frac{1}{10}\,\frac{1}{10}}$

6. $\boxed{\frac{1}{6}\,\frac{1}{6}}$ $\boxed{\frac{1}{6}\,\frac{1}{6}\,\frac{1}{6}}$

_____   _____   _____

Add. You may use models if you wish.

7. $\frac{3}{5} + \frac{1}{5} =$ _____

8. $\frac{1}{3} + \frac{1}{3} =$ _____

9. $\frac{2}{4} + \frac{1}{4} =$ _____

10. $\frac{4}{6} + \frac{1}{6} =$ _____

11. $\frac{3}{12} + \frac{5}{12} =$ _____

12. $\frac{1}{10} + \frac{8}{10} =$ _____

13. $\frac{4}{8} + \frac{1}{8} =$ _____

14. $\frac{3}{8} + \frac{3}{8} =$ _____

15. $\frac{5}{6} + \frac{5}{6} =$ _____

16. $\frac{5}{8} + \frac{9}{8} =$ _____

17. $\frac{2}{10} + \frac{6}{10} =$ _____

18. $\frac{7}{12} + \frac{1}{12} =$ _____

19. $\frac{2}{12} + \frac{4}{12} =$ _____

20. $\frac{5}{6} + \frac{4}{6} =$ _____

21. $\frac{5}{8} + \frac{5}{8} =$ _____

22. $\begin{array}{r} \frac{8}{12} \\ + \frac{3}{12} \\ \hline \end{array}$

23. $\begin{array}{r} \frac{2}{8} \\ + \frac{3}{8} \\ \hline \end{array}$

24. $\begin{array}{r} \frac{2}{3} \\ + \frac{1}{3} \\ \hline \end{array}$

25. $\begin{array}{r} \frac{1}{6} \\ + \frac{5}{6} \\ \hline \end{array}$

26. $\begin{array}{r} \frac{3}{8} \\ + \frac{1}{8} \\ \hline \end{array}$

27. $\begin{array}{r} \frac{3}{10} \\ + \frac{5}{10} \\ \hline \end{array}$

McGraw-Hill School Division

ADD FRACTIONS

Add. Write the sum in simplest form.

1. $\frac{1}{8}$
$+\frac{2}{8}$

2. $\frac{3}{8}$
$+\frac{5}{8}$

3. $\frac{5}{8}$
$+\frac{5}{8}$

4. $\frac{5}{12}$
$+\frac{1}{12}$

5. $\frac{1}{3}$
$+\frac{2}{3}$

6. $\frac{2}{4}$
$+\frac{3}{4}$

7. $\frac{3}{5}$
$+\frac{2}{5}$

8. $\frac{3}{8}$
$+\frac{2}{8}$

9. $\frac{7}{10}$
$+\frac{5}{10}$

10. $\frac{2}{7}$
$+\frac{6}{7}$

11. $\frac{7}{9}$
$+\frac{2}{9}$

12. $\frac{3}{10}$
$+\frac{2}{10}$

13. $\frac{1}{9} + \frac{4}{9} =$ _____

14. $\frac{2}{3} + \frac{1}{3} =$ _____

15. $\frac{1}{12} + \frac{5}{12} =$ _____

16. $\frac{2}{5} + \frac{4}{5} =$ _____

17. $\frac{3}{8} + \frac{5}{8} =$ _____

18. $\frac{3}{4} + \frac{2}{4} =$ _____

19. $\frac{2}{10} + \frac{3}{10} + \frac{6}{10} =$ _____

20. $\frac{1}{8} + \frac{5}{8} + \frac{3}{8} =$ _____

21. $\frac{6}{11} + \frac{3}{11} + \frac{1}{11} =$ _____

22. $\frac{2}{7} + \frac{1}{7} + \frac{4}{7} =$ _____

Find the perimeter of the rectangle.

23.

$\frac{1}{4}$ yd

_____

24.
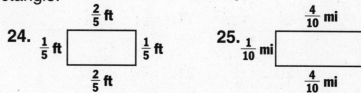
$\frac{2}{5}$ ft
$\frac{1}{5}$ ft $\frac{1}{5}$ ft
$\frac{2}{5}$ ft

_____

25.
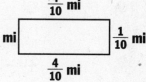
$\frac{4}{10}$ mi
$\frac{1}{10}$ mi $\frac{1}{10}$ mi
$\frac{4}{10}$ mi

_____

Solve.

26. You need at least $1\frac{1}{4}$ yd of paper for a mural. You tape together 2 pieces that are $\frac{3}{4}$ yd each. Is the paper long enough? How long is it?

_____

27. You decide to make some home-made clay. The recipe calls for $\frac{2}{3}$ cup of flour. What if you want to double the recipe? How much flour will you need?

_____

McGraw-Hill School Division

Name:

SUBTRACT FRACTIONS

Write the subtraction sentence that each model shows.

1. $\frac{1}{4}$ $\frac{1}{4}$ $\frac{1}{4}$

_____

2. $\frac{1}{3}$ $\frac{1}{3}$

_____

3. $\frac{1}{5}$ $\frac{1}{5}$ $\frac{1}{5}$ $\frac{1}{5}$

_____

4. $\frac{1}{10}$ $\frac{1}{10}$ $\frac{1}{10}$ $\frac{1}{10}$ $\frac{1}{10}$ $\frac{1}{10}$ $\frac{1}{10}$

_____

5. $\frac{1}{12}$ $\frac{1}{12}$ $\frac{1}{12}$ $\frac{1}{12}$ $\frac{1}{12}$

_____

6. $\frac{1}{6}$ $\frac{1}{6}$ $\frac{1}{6}$ $\frac{1}{6}$ $\frac{1}{6}$

_____

Subtract. Write the difference in simplest form.

7. $\frac{5}{6} - \frac{4}{6} =$ _____

8. $\frac{5}{8} - \frac{4}{8} =$ _____

9. $\frac{4}{5} - \frac{3}{5} =$ _____

10. $\frac{3}{3} - \frac{1}{3} =$ _____

11. $\frac{5}{8} - \frac{5}{8} =$ _____

12. $\frac{3}{4} - \frac{1}{4} =$ _____

13. $\frac{7}{9} - \frac{1}{9} =$ _____

14. $\frac{7}{12} - \frac{3}{12} =$ _____

15. $\frac{15}{13} - \frac{9}{13} =$ _____

16. $\frac{9}{14} - \frac{7}{14} =$ _____

17. $\frac{9}{15} - \frac{3}{15} =$ _____

18. $\frac{9}{18} - \frac{7}{18} =$ _____

19. $\frac{7}{10}$ $- \frac{3}{10}$

20. $\frac{3}{6}$ $- \frac{2}{6}$

21. $\frac{6}{7}$ $- \frac{1}{7}$

22. $\frac{5}{8}$ $- \frac{1}{8}$

23. $\frac{2}{5}$ $- \frac{2}{5}$

24. $\frac{7}{10}$ $- \frac{2}{10}$

Algebra Ring the letter of the number that completes the number sentence.

25. $\frac{7}{8} -$ _____ $= \frac{5}{8}$ **a.** $\frac{1}{8}$ **b.** $\frac{1}{2}$ **c.** $\frac{2}{4}$ **d.** $\frac{2}{8}$

26. $\frac{9}{10} -$ _____ $= \frac{1}{2}$ **a.** $\frac{5}{10}$ **b.** $\frac{4}{10}$ **c.** $\frac{8}{10}$ **d.** $\frac{1}{2}$

McGraw-Hill School Division

SUBTRACT FRACTIONS

Subtract. Write the difference in simplest form.

1. $\frac{3}{4}$
    $-\frac{2}{4}$

2. $\frac{7}{11}$
    $-\frac{5}{11}$

3. $\frac{6}{7}$
    $-\frac{1}{7}$

4. $\frac{3}{4}$
    $-\frac{1}{4}$

5. $\frac{6}{12}$
    $-\frac{6}{12}$

6. $\frac{11}{12}$
    $-\frac{7}{12}$

7. $\frac{9}{10}$
    $-\frac{7}{10}$

8. $\frac{9}{14}$
    $-\frac{2}{14}$

9. $\frac{6}{12}$
    $-\frac{3}{12}$

10. $\frac{8}{9}$
    $-\frac{5}{9}$

11. $\frac{5}{8}$
    $-\frac{1}{8}$

12. $\frac{9}{10}$
    $-\frac{3}{10}$

13. $\frac{11}{12} - \frac{3}{12} =$ _____

14. $\frac{4}{5} - \frac{1}{5} =$ _____

15. $\frac{7}{18} - \frac{1}{18} =$ _____

16. $\frac{5}{7} - \frac{1}{7} =$ _____

17. $\frac{7}{12} - \frac{6}{12} =$ _____

18. $\frac{7}{10} - \frac{6}{10} =$ _____

19. $\frac{9}{15} - \frac{1}{15} =$ _____

20. $\frac{6}{7} - \frac{4}{7} =$ _____

21. $\frac{9}{16} - \frac{9}{16} =$ _____

Algebra Write <, >, or =.

22. $\frac{3}{4} - \frac{1}{4} \bigcirc \frac{1}{2}$

23. $\frac{9}{10} - \frac{4}{10} \bigcirc \frac{1}{4}$

24. $\frac{11}{12} - \frac{4}{12} \bigcirc \frac{1}{2}$

25. $\frac{6}{12} - \frac{3}{12} \bigcirc \frac{1}{2}$

26. $\frac{4}{7} - \frac{2}{7} \bigcirc \frac{3}{7}$

27. $\frac{8}{9} - \frac{2}{9} \bigcirc \frac{1}{3}$

28. $\frac{10}{12} - \frac{2}{12} \bigcirc \frac{2}{3}$

29. $\frac{7}{8} - \frac{3}{8} \bigcirc \frac{1}{4}$

30. $\frac{13}{16} - \frac{9}{16} \bigcirc \frac{1}{4}$

31. $\frac{4}{5} - \frac{1}{5} \bigcirc \frac{7}{8}$

32. $\frac{8}{9} - \frac{5}{9} \bigcirc \frac{1}{3}$

33. $\frac{5}{7} - \frac{4}{7} \bigcirc \frac{1}{2}$

Solve.

34. At lunch, you cut an apple into 4 parts and eat 3 of the parts. What fraction of the apple don't you eat?

35. For breakfast, lunch, and dinner, you will drink equal parts of a quart of milk. How much of the quart is left after lunch?

_____   _____

FIND A COMMON DENOMINATOR

Name the common denominator.

1. $\frac{1}{2}$ and $\frac{1}{4}$ _____

2. $\frac{1}{4}$ and $\frac{3}{8}$ _____

3. $\frac{3}{9}$ and $\frac{1}{3}$ _____

4. $\frac{5}{6}$ and $\frac{1}{3}$ _____

5. $\frac{5}{10}$ and $\frac{2}{5}$ _____

6. $\frac{1}{2}$ and $\frac{1}{8}$ _____

7. $\frac{3}{4}$ and $\frac{2}{8}$ _____

8. $\frac{3}{4}$ and $\frac{2}{3}$ _____

9. $\frac{3}{4}$ and $\frac{5}{6}$ _____

10. $\frac{1}{3}$ and $\frac{1}{2}$ _____

11. $\frac{1}{6}$ and $\frac{3}{4}$ _____

12. $\frac{5}{8}$ and $\frac{2}{3}$ _____

13. $\frac{1}{10}$ and $\frac{2}{5}$ _____

14. $\frac{2}{3}$ and $\frac{3}{9}$ _____

15. $\frac{1}{4}$ and $\frac{1}{5}$ _____

16. $\frac{3}{5}$ and $\frac{2}{3}$ _____

17. $\frac{2}{7}$ and $\frac{1}{3}$ _____

18. $\frac{1}{9}$ and $\frac{5}{6}$ _____

19. $\frac{1}{4}$ and $\frac{1}{7}$ _____

20. $\frac{2}{5}$ and $\frac{1}{15}$ _____

21. $\frac{3}{7}$ and $\frac{4}{5}$ _____

Write as equivalent fractions with common denominators.

22. $\frac{1}{4}$ and $\frac{2}{8}$ _____

23. $\frac{3}{6}$ and $\frac{2}{3}$ _____

24. $\frac{1}{5}$ and $\frac{2}{10}$ _____

25. $\frac{2}{5}$ and $\frac{10}{15}$ _____

26. $\frac{5}{9}$ and $\frac{1}{3}$ _____

27. $\frac{3}{8}$ and $\frac{1}{4}$ _____

28. $\frac{1}{3}$ and $\frac{5}{12}$ _____

29. $\frac{1}{2}$ and $\frac{3}{8}$ _____

30. $\frac{3}{4}$ and $\frac{9}{12}$ _____

31. $\frac{3}{5}$ and $\frac{6}{25}$ _____

32. $\frac{1}{3}$ and $\frac{3}{5}$ _____

33. $\frac{1}{3}$ and $\frac{1}{7}$ _____

34. $\frac{1}{2}$ and $\frac{4}{5}$ _____

35. $\frac{4}{9}$ and $\frac{1}{2}$ _____

36. $\frac{1}{7}$ and $\frac{1}{2}$ _____

37. $\frac{2}{9}$ and $\frac{5}{6}$ _____

38. $\frac{3}{8}$ and $\frac{1}{6}$ _____

39. $\frac{3}{4}$ and $\frac{5}{7}$ _____

ADD AND SUBTRACT FRACTIONS WITH UNLIKE DENOMINATORS

Use the models to complete the number sentence.

1.

| $\frac{1}{3}$ | $\frac{1}{3}$ | $\frac{1}{6}$ |

| $\frac{1}{6}$ | $\frac{1}{6}$ | $\frac{1}{6}$ | $\frac{1}{6}$ |

$\frac{2}{3} + \frac{1}{6} =$

$\frac{\square}{6} + \frac{1}{6} = \frac{5}{6}$

2.

| $\frac{1}{4}$ | $\frac{1}{8}$ | $\frac{1}{8}$ | $\frac{1}{8}$ |

| $\frac{1}{8}$ | $\frac{1}{8}$ |

$\frac{1}{4} + \frac{3}{8} =$

$\frac{\square}{8} + \frac{3}{8} = \frac{5}{8}$

3.

| $\frac{1}{10}$ | $\frac{1}{10}$ | $\frac{1}{10}$ | $\frac{1}{10}$ | $\frac{1}{10}$ | $\frac{1}{10}$ | $\frac{1}{10}$ |

| $\frac{1}{5}$ | $\frac{1}{5}$ |

$\frac{7}{10} - \frac{2}{5} =$

$\frac{7}{10} - \frac{\square}{10} = \frac{3}{10}$

Find the equivalent fraction. Then add or subtract. Write the sum or difference in simplest form.

4. $\frac{1}{8} \rightarrow \frac{\square}{8}$

$+ \frac{3}{4} \rightarrow + \frac{\square}{8}$

_____

$\frac{\square}{8}$

5. $\frac{1}{3} \rightarrow \frac{\square}{12}$

$+ \frac{7}{12} \rightarrow + \frac{\square}{12}$

_____

$\frac{\square}{12}$

6. $\frac{4}{5} \rightarrow \frac{\square}{10}$

$- \frac{2}{10} \rightarrow - \frac{\square}{10}$

_____

$\frac{\square}{10}$

7. $\frac{9}{15} \rightarrow \frac{\square}{15}$

$- \frac{3}{5} \rightarrow - \frac{\square}{15}$

_____

$\frac{\square}{15}$

Add or subtract using any method. Write the sum or difference in simplest form.

8. $\frac{6}{10}$
$- \frac{1}{5}$
___

9. $\frac{3}{4}$
$+ \frac{1}{6}$
___

10. $\frac{7}{8}$
$- \frac{3}{4}$
___

11. $\frac{9}{15}$
$+ \frac{2}{3}$
___

12. $\frac{9}{10}$
$- \frac{3}{5}$
___

13. $\frac{7}{12}$
$+ \frac{2}{6}$
___

14. $\frac{1}{8} + \frac{1}{2} =$ _____

15. $\frac{1}{2} + \frac{1}{4} =$ _____

16. $\frac{1}{3} + \frac{1}{6} =$ _____

17. $\frac{1}{5} + \frac{1}{10} =$ _____

18. $\frac{1}{3} + \frac{3}{5} =$ _____

19. $\frac{1}{8} + \frac{3}{4} =$ _____

20. $\frac{2}{3} + \frac{5}{9} =$ _____

21. $\frac{1}{2} + \frac{1}{9} =$ _____

22. $\frac{7}{12} - \frac{1}{4} =$ _____

McGraw-Hill School Division

PROBLEM-SOLVING STRATEGY: DRAW A PICTURE

✔	Read
✔	Plan
✔	Solve
✔	Look Back

Solve using the draw-a-picture strategy.

1. In your kitchen cupboard, $\frac{1}{4}$ of a shelf has beans, $\frac{1}{2}$ has soup, and $\frac{1}{8}$ has peas. What fraction of the shelf is left for carrots?

_____

2. On another shelf, $\frac{1}{3}$ has baby food, $\frac{1}{4}$ has apple sauce, $\frac{1}{6}$ has peaches. How much of this shelf is left for jars of strawberry jam?

_____

3. You make a row of 4 spices. The salt is between the pepper and the nutmeg. The nutmeg is at the end of one row. Where is the cinnamon? In what order do you have the 4 spices?

_____

_____

4. On a shelf, you stack rice, cereal, napkins, bread, and crackers. The cereal is on top of the crackers. The bread is above the cereal but below the rice, which is under the napkins. Draw the stack.

_____

_____

Solve using any method.

5. You have 2 melons for 8 people. You plan to cut the melons in thirds. Will you have enough pieces? What else could you do?

_____

6. There are 2 pints in a quart and 4 quarts in a gallon. What part of a gallon do you drink when you have 1 pint? How about 1 quart?

_____

7. You buy 25 cans of peaches at $1.22 a can. You have $30 in bills and 4 quarters. Will that be enough? Can you still buy 2 more cans?

_____

8. There are 4 people in your family. They each eat an apple a day. Use mental math to estimate about how many apples that is in a month.

_____

McGraw-Hill School Division

ADD AND SUBTRACT MIXED NUMBERS

Ring the answer that tells what each model represents.

1.

| 1 | | $\frac{1}{4}$ |

+

| 1 | | $\frac{1}{4}$ | $\frac{1}{4}$ |

a. $1\frac{1}{4} + 1\frac{1}{4}$ **b.** $1\frac{1}{4} + 1\frac{2}{4}$

c. $1\frac{2}{4} + 1\frac{3}{4}$ **d.** $2\frac{1}{4} + 1\frac{1}{4}$

2.

| ✗ |

| 1 |

| $\frac{1}{5}$ | $\frac{1}{5}$ | $\frac{1}{5}$ |

a. $2\frac{3}{5} + 1\frac{1}{5}$ **b.** $2\frac{3}{5} - 1\frac{1}{5}$

c. $2\frac{1}{3} - 1\frac{1}{5}$ **d.** $2\frac{1}{3} + 1\frac{1}{5}$

Algebra Complete the tables. Write the answers in simplest form.

3.

Rule: Add $4\frac{1}{3}$.				
$\frac{1}{3}$	$\frac{2}{3}$	$\frac{3}{3}$	$\frac{4}{3}$	$\frac{5}{3}$

4.

Rule: Subtract $1\frac{3}{15}$.				
$3\frac{5}{15}$	$3\frac{6}{15}$	$3\frac{7}{15}$	$3\frac{8}{15}$	$3\frac{9}{15}$

Add or subtract. Use fraction strips if you want. Regroup and simplify when necessary.

5. $2\frac{1}{3} + 2\frac{1}{3} =$ _____   **6.** $1\frac{5}{8} + \frac{2}{8} =$ _____   **7.** $3\frac{1}{2} + 5\frac{1}{2} =$ _____

8. $\quad 1\frac{2}{2}$ **9.** $\quad 2\frac{3}{8}$ **10.** $\quad 6\frac{7}{8}$ **11.** $\quad 2\frac{7}{15}$ **12.** $\quad 5\frac{9}{10}$ **13.** $\quad 6\frac{8}{9}$

$\quad\quad -\frac{1}{2}$ $+1\frac{5}{8}$ $-1\frac{3}{8}$ $+\frac{9}{15}$ $+3\frac{7}{10}$ $-2\frac{2}{9}$

PROBLEM SOLVING: CHOOSE THE OPERATION

Solve. Tell which operation(s) you used.

1. Your class is writing notes using invisible ink. You write 4 notes each day. How many notes do you write by the fifth day?

_____

2. It takes about $\frac{1}{4}$ c of invisible ink to write 3 notes. How much invisible ink would you use to write 12 notes?

_____

3. Your class is using baking powder and water to make the invisible ink. There is $\frac{1}{4}$ of one can of baking powder and $\frac{5}{6}$ of another can. How much more than one can is that?

_____

4. Thirteen students have each written 48 notes, 10 students have written 15, and 8 have written 12. If the class goal is 1,000 notes, how many more have to be written?

_____

Solve using any method.

5. The fourth grade spends 25 minutes each day writing in a journal, 5 minutes for schedule writing, and 2 minutes for joke, riddle, or skit writing. How many minutes of writing is that in 38 school days?

_____

6. You draw a poster for a writing contest. One fourth of the poster is for contest rules, $\frac{1}{12}$ is for previous winners, and $\frac{1}{6}$ for suggested titles. What fraction of the poster is still blank? Draw it.

_____

7. You fold paper to write one sentence in each section. Complete the table to show how many sections are created with each fold.

Folds	1	2	3	4	5
Sections	2				

8. The PTA awards your class $100 for your writing program. You buy 16 boxes of colored pencils at $3.25 each and 8 packages of paper at $4.95. About how much of the $100 is left over?

_____

McGraw-Hill School Division

● DECIMALS LESS THAN 1

Write a decimal for the part that is shaded.

1.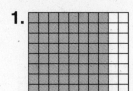

2.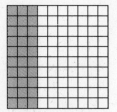

3.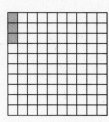

4.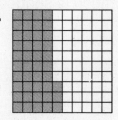

_____ _____ _____ _____

Write a decimal and a word name.

5. $\frac{9}{10}$ _____

6. $\frac{8}{10}$ _____

7. $\frac{6}{10}$ _____

8. $\frac{7}{10}$ _____

9. $\frac{4}{10}$ _____

10. $\frac{1}{10}$ _____

11. $\frac{6}{100}$ _____

12. $\frac{3}{100}$ _____

13. $\frac{5}{100}$ _____

14. $\frac{4}{100}$ _____

15. $\frac{82}{100}$ _____

16. $\frac{65}{100}$ _____

17. $\frac{27}{100}$ _____

18. $\frac{1}{100}$ _____

19. $\frac{56}{100}$ _____

20. $\frac{13}{100}$ _____

Draw a line to match a money amount to its word name.

21. three tenths of a dollar   **a.** $0.25

22. one hundredth of a dollar   **b.** $0.60

23. six tenths of a dollar   **c.** $0.01

24. twenty-five hundredths of a dollar   **d.** $0.30

25. eleven hundredths of a dollar   **e.** $0.11

DECIMALS GREATER THAN 1

Write a mixed number and a decimal to tell how much is shaded.

1.

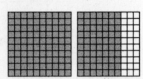

_____

2.

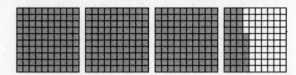

_____

Write a decimal and a word name.

3. $1\frac{9}{10}$

_____

4. $1\frac{9}{100}$

_____

5. $3\frac{2}{10}$

_____

6. $3\frac{2}{100}$

_____

7. $5\frac{7}{10}$

_____

8. $6\frac{5}{100}$

_____

9. $4\frac{3}{10}$

_____

10. $5\frac{7}{100}$

_____

11. $2\frac{9}{10}$

_____

12. $4\frac{3}{100}$

_____

Solve.

13. Out of 100 backpacks at a store, 47 have leather trim. What decimal shows the number of backpacks with leather trim?

_____

14. Out of 100 handbags in a store, 60 are black. What decimal shows the number of handbags that are black?

_____

COMPARE AND ORDER DECIMALS

Compare. Write >, <, or =.

1. 0.1 ◯ 0.01   **2.** 9.09 ◯ 0.90   **3.** 0.15 ◯ 0.51   **4.** 6.2 ◯ 6.20

5. 5.02 ◯ 5.20   **6.** 0.93 ◯ 0.39   **7.** 3.03 ◯ 3.30   **8.** 7.64 ◯ 7.46

9. 2.22 ◯ 2.21   **10.** 1.11 ◯ 11.11   **11.** 1.1 ◯ 1.10   **12.** $1.01 ◯ $1.10

13. $7.44 ◯ $4.77   **14.** 1.00 ◯ 0.11   **15.** 4.55 ◯ 5.45   **16.** 16.11 ◯ 61.11

17. 3.33 ◯ 3.13   **18.** 4.04 ◯ 4.14   **19.** 7.08 ◯ 7.8   **20.** 8.07 ◯ 8.07

21. 29.5 ◯ 29.35   **22.** 0.38 ◯ 0.33   **23.** 14.4 ◯ 14.04   **24.** 5.12 ◯ 2.15

Write in order from least to greatest.

25. 1.7, 1.0, 0.9   **26.** 0.7, 0.3, 1.3   **27.** 3.52, 3.25, 3.11

_____   _____   _____

28. 5.07, 4.07, 6.07   **29.** 8.4, 8.04, 8.14   **30.** 2.60, 12.60, 2.66

_____   _____   _____

31. 8.14, 9.62, 7.20   **32.** 2.19, 2.91, 2.09   **33.** 2.01, 2.00, 2.10

_____   _____   _____

34. 1.04, 1.44, 1.24   **35.** 0.77, 0.07, 0.71   **36.** 0.99, 0.09, 0.90

_____   _____   _____

Solve.

37. An oak tree is 9.2 meters tall. An elm tree is 9.6 meters tall. A maple tree is 9.4 meters tall. Which tree is the tallest?

38. The maple tree grew 1.05 meters last year and 1.5 meters the year before. In which year did the tree grow more?

_____   _____

PROBLEM-SOLVING STRATEGY: SOLVE A SIMPLER PROBLEM

✔ Read
✔ Plan
✔ Solve
✔ Look Back

Solve by the solving-a-simpler-problem strategy. Explain how you could use a simpler problem.

1. Kenny baby-sits for $2\frac{3}{4}$ hours each Monday, Wednesday, and Friday. How many hours a week does he baby-sit?

_____

_____

2. Joy baby-sits from 4:30 P.M. to 5:15 P.M. for 4 days each week. She is paid $3 an hour. How much is she paid in a week?

_____

_____

3. Joy buys 3 coloring books for $0.79 each, and 2 boxes of crayons for $1.19 each. How much does she spend?

_____

_____

4. Joy will buy new boots when she has saved $50 from baby-sitting. So far, she has saved $3.50, $16.25, $7.90, and $12.25. How much more does she need?

_____

_____

Solve using any method.

5. Joy plans activities for 180 minutes of baby-sitting. She spends equal amounts of time on lunch, watching cartoons, napping, drawing, and playing games. How much time does she spend on each activity?

_____

6. Joy and Kenny compare the number of baby-sitting hours in one week. Joy says she baby-sat $4\frac{1}{2}$ hours. Kenny says he baby-sat 4 hours and 30 minutes. Write a number sentence to compare the hours they baby-sat.

_____

MENTAL MATH: ESTIMATE SUMS AND DIFFERENCES

Estimate. Round to the nearest whole number.

1. 2.3 + 1.5 _____   **2.** 1.9 + 1.0 _____   **3.** 1.2 + 2.2 _____

4. 6.3 + 0.1 _____   **5.** 5.6 − 1.1 _____   **6.** 10.7 − 8.5 _____

7. 3.4 − 1.0 _____   **8.** 5.5 − 1.6 _____   **9.** 7.34 + 1.55 _____

10. 8.84 − 2.14 _____   **11.** 2.11 + 4.11 _____   **12.** 9.3 − 7.9 _____

13. 12 − 2.5 _____   **14.** 1.9 − 1.1 _____   **15.** 2.95 + 0.5 _____

16. 0.99 + 0.99 + 0.99 _____   **17.** 2.1 + 3.2 + 1.1 _____

18. 2.3 + 3.4 + 1.2 _____   **19.** 5.88 + 4.11 + 7.02 _____

20. 7.14 + 9.2 + 8.1 _____   **21.** 6.01 + 3.8 + 4.3 _____

22. 7.45 + 3.81 + 2.52 _____   **23.** 9.20 + 9.10 + 9.10 _____

Estimate. Round to the nearest dollar.

24. $2.23 + $1.19 _____   **25.** $4.75 + $3.50 _____

26. $0.70 + $0.07 _____   **27.** $1.49 + $11.95 _____

28. $15.25 − $9.95 _____   **29.** $43.29 − $8.07 _____

Solve.

30. Duane gives his plant 1.5 measures of plant food each week for 3 weeks and then 1.25 measures each week for 2 weeks. About how many whole measures is that?

31. Duane buys plant food for $4.95 and a new watering can. He gives the clerk $20 and gets $9.65 in change. About how much does the watering can cost?

_____   _____

ADD AND SUBTRACT DECIMALS

Use decimal squares to add or subtract.

1.	0.2 + 0.3	2.	0.5 + 0.6	3.	1.2 + 2.1	4.	5.9 + 2.3	5.	7.2 + 6.8
6.	6.36 + 1.92	7.	5.79 + 2.90	8.	8.28 + 5.93	9.	1.87 + 0.99	10.	3.05 + 4.55
11.	0.9 − 0.3	12.	9.3 − 5.2	13.	9.1 − 5.2	14.	1.75 − 0.28	15.	8.24 − 1.33
16.	3.25 − 2.91	17.	1.19 − 0.27	18.	4.21 − 2.50	19.	9.11 − 1.31	20.	0.55 − 0.19
21.	0.9 − 0.8	22.	1.9 + 0.8	23.	1.84 − 0.15	24.	2.11 − 0.22	25.	2.11 + 0.22
26.	1.28 + 5.57	27.	3.44 + 2.22	28.	2.03 + 1.99	29.	8.53 − 0.73	30.	5.55 − 2.59
31.	8.04 + 0.89	32.	8.64 − 0.89	33.	2.05 − 0.91	34.	2.09 − 1.55	35.	7.56 + 1.05
36.	3.34 + 1.29	37.	7.23 − 2.45	38.	5.23 + 2.19	39.	2.95 + 4.87	40.	3.43 − 2.91
41.	8.20 − 2.18	42.	6.32 + 5.97	43.	4.87 + 1.23	44.	8.32 − 6.51	45.	1.07 − 0.67

McGraw-Hill School Division

ADD DECIMALS

Add using any method. Remember to estimate.

1.	2.	3.	4.	5.	6.
0.28	0.15	0.50	0.55	1.50	3.27
+ 0.19	+ 0.59	+ 0.50	+ 0.55	+ 1.50	+ 2.81

7.	8.	9.	10.	11.	12.
5.77	4.21	3.21	$6.29	18.05	2.45
+ 1.33	+ 0.88	+ 0.59	+ 2.99	+ 7.29	+ 19.50

13.	14.	15.	16.	17.	18.
0.94	12.25	23.55	12.15	16.05	48.75
+ 21.6	+ 0.75	+ 9.4	+ 8.2	+ 4.15	+ 6.42

19.	20.	21.	22.	23.	24.
1.17	16.50	5.27	$9.03	$1.50	$8.95
+ 29.97	+ 8.40	13.05	27.50	0.05	24.50
		+ 9.8	+ 8.40	+ 15.95	+ 13.00

25. $6.5 + 0.42 =$ _____

26. $8.6 + 9.4 =$ _____

27. $12.25 + 12.55 =$ _____

28. $9.55 + 2.01 + 1.4 =$ _____

29. $1.50 + 1.50 + 1.50 =$ _____

30. $28.4 + 3.55 + 7.55 =$ _____

31. $1.72 + 2.27 + 7.12 =$ _____

32. $1.72 + 4.68 + 1.10 =$ _____

33. $9.57 + 4.51 + 6.3 =$ _____

34. $24.53 + 1.78 + 3.45 =$ _____

Solve.

35. At the post office, Lauren bought stamps for $2.47 and envelopes for $1.29. How much did she spend?

36. At the hardware store, Lauren bought packing tape for $1.97 and mailing cartons for $6.35. How much did she spend?

_____   _____

SUBTRACT DECIMALS

Subtract using any method. Remember to estimate.

1. 0.5 − 0.2	**2.** 5.7 − 0.9	**3.** 8.1 − 3.2	**4.** 7.3 − 2.7	**5.** 6.8 − 0.9	**6.** 0.57 − 0.18
7. 0.66 − 0.12	**8.** 5.00 − 2.55	**9.** 4.03 − 2.11	**10.** 2.00 − 0.65	**11.** 8.00 − 0.05	**12.** 8.00 − 3.50
13. 8.00 − 5.00	**14.** 8.00 −1.5	**15.** 8.00 − 2.15	**16.** 7.43 − 3.5	**17.** 9.54 − 0.35	**18.** 6.97 − 1.5
19. 8.32 − 1.05	**20.** 5.09 − 0.05	**21.** $9.37 − 6.28	**22.** $10.00 − 1.99	**23.** $5.35 − 1.75	**24.** $9.05 − 6.20

25. 8.5 − 2.3 = _____

26. 9.4 − 1.05 = _____

27. 6.6 − 2.09 = _____

28. 7.01 − 2.55 = _____

29. 4.22 − 1.97 = _____

30. 7.61 − 6.99 = _____

31. $5.75 − $1.09 = _____

32. $3.57 − $1.19 = _____

33. $7.75 − $0.80 = _____

34. $25 − $1.05 = _____

Solve.

35. At a bookstore, you buy a small dictionary for $6.15 and pay with a $10 bill. What change do you get back?

36. You buy books for $2.05, $7.50, and $3.75, and pay $0.87 in tax. What is your change from a $20 bill?

_____

_____

PROBLEM SOLVING: WRITE A NUMBER SENTENCE

✔ Read
✔ Plan
✔ Solve
✔ Look Back

Write a number sentence to solve.

1. Write a number sentence to show the total kilometers hiked by the club in 6 weeks.

_____

2. Write a number sentence to show the difference between the greatest and least number of kilometers hiked.

_____

SATURDAY HIKING CLUB	
Week 1	2.30 km
Week 2	2.05 km
Week 3	3.05 km
Week 4	4.50 km
Week 5	4.95 km
Week 6	5.50 km

3. The club wanted to hike $\frac{1}{2}$ kilometer more than they did in Week 4. Write a number sentence to show that total.

_____

4. Between which 2 weeks did the hiking club increase their hike by one kilometer? Write a number sentence.

_____

Solve using any method.

5. During a long weekend, the club hiked $1\frac{1}{4}$ kilometers on Friday, $2\frac{1}{6}$ kilometers on Saturday, and $2\frac{1}{4}$ kilometers on Sunday. How many kilometers did they hike over the weekend?

_____

6. The club plans to hike 10 kilometers in the winter. So far, they have hiked 3.5, 2.75, and 1.55 kilometers. How many more kilometers do they need to reach their goal?

_____

7. By holding fundraisers the hiking club has made $195.25, $107.50, $83.25, and $66. What was the average amount of profit?

_____

8. The fastest hiker in the club can travel 1.6 kilometers in 30 minutes. How far might she be able to travel in 90 minutes?

_____